Field Trip Theme-A-Saurus

The Great Big Book of Field Trips and Related Teaching Themes

Written by JOANN SPEARS

Developmental Editor

MARSHA ELYN WRIGHT

Illustrated by MARILYNN BARR

Totline® Publications
A Division of Frank Schaffer Publications, Inc.
Torrance, California

Editorial Director: Stephanie Oberc-Garcia
Developmental Editor: Marsha Elyn Wright
Contributing Editors: Kathy Zaun, Mina McMullin, Jean Warren
Editorial Assistant: Mary Newmaster
Graphic Designer (Interior): Jill Kaufman
Graphic Designer (Cover): Brenda Mann Harrison
Cover Illustration: Jeremy Eaton
Production Manager: Janie Schmidt

Theme-A-Saurus® is a registered trademark of
Warren Publishing House, Inc.

Published by Totline® Publications
A Division of Frank Schaffer Publications
23740 Hawthorne Blvd.
Torrance, CA 90505

Contents

Field Trip Tips 4

Traditional Field Trips 9

Field Trip Alternatives 14

Aquarium 18

Bakery 22

Bank 26

Beach 30

Bird Watching Area 34

Botanical Garden 38

Bus Station, Train Station,
    or Airport 42

Clock Shop 46

Construction Site.............................50

Dairy 54

Dentist Office..................................58

Farm 62

Feed Store..66

Fire Department 70

Florist 74

Grocery Store...................................78

Hospital 82

Kite Store 86

Lumberyard.....................................90

Music Shop 94

Neighborhood.................................98

Newspaper Office..........................102

Optometrist 106

Park 110

Pet Store 114

Plant Nursery 118

Post Office 122

Service Station 126

Shell Shop 130

Television Station 134

Veterinary Hospital 138

Weather Station 142

Wildlife Refuge 146

X-ray Lab 150

Zoo 154

Thank-You Posters
    for Any Field Trip 158

Parent Letter 159

Name Tag Patterns 160

Field Trip Tips

Field trips are an important part of a child's education. A well-planned trip is a great adventure! Field trips introduce children to their community and give children a chance to learn firsthand how things work.

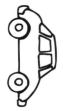

Sometimes school rules and regulations make planning a field trip a real challenge! This guide provides a complete list of steps needed to plan and organize a field trip for children three years old and older. It also lists ideas for traditional field trips and "backyard" field trips that feature guest speakers with special equipment.

10 Steps for Planning a Fun Field Trip

You may decide that traditional field trips are the best experience for your children. These trips require the most planning and preparation time. Here are 10 steps to help you better organize a traditional field trip:

1. Visit the site of the field trip before announcing the trip.

2. Tell the person in charge what you want the children to see and to learn.

3. Discuss dates and times for the trip. Set an alternate date in case bad weather or other problems postpone the trip.

4. Write down the address, contact person, telephone number, and dates. Store this information for future trips. Call the day before the trip to confirm your arrival.

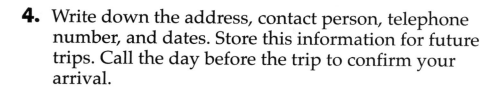

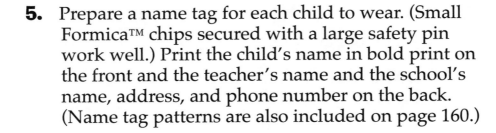

5. Prepare a name tag for each child to wear. (Small Formica™ chips secured with a large safety pin work well.) Print the child's name in bold print on the front and the teacher's name and the school's name, address, and phone number on the back. (Name tag patterns are also included on page 160.)

6. If you depend on parents to drive personal cars, prepare a file for your records that includes liability insurance information, number of working seat belts, and days parents are available to drive and their telephone numbers. (It is helpful to include information about car phones and car phone numbers.)

7. Prepare maps that include the planned route and the actual name, address, and telephone number of the field trip location. Give one to each driver.

8. For each driver, provide a copy of emergency information that includes parental consent for emergency medical care.

9. Collect first-aid supplies and emergency equipment required by licensing standards.

10. Teach children the Field Trip Rules. (See page 6 for a list of rules.)

Field Trip Rules

🚌 Wear your name tag and do not try to remove it.

🚌 Stay with the group.

🚌 Wear your seat belt until the driver tells you to take it off.

🚌 Keep your hands away from the car doors and windows.

🚌 Use a soft voice in the car and on the trip.

🚌 Use your best manners.

🚌 Be a good listener.

🚌 Raise your hand to ask a question.

🚌 Ask questions that begin with words like who, what, how, and why.

🚌 Say "Thank you" when you leave.

Staff and Volunteers

Be sure at least one adult has current training in first aid and CPR for children. Take time to train staff, volunteers, and parents in the facility's policies and procedures. The following child/staff ratio is suggested as a minimum standard; compare these with your licensing standards:

3-year-olds: 1 adult to 6 children

4-year-olds: 1 adult to 8 children

5-year-olds: 1 adult to 10 children

6+-year-olds: 1 adult to 12 children

Equipment Check List

Each vehicle transporting children should take along a large plastic basket or crate of safety equipment. If this is an outdoor trip, you might want to pack the materials in a backpack. Collect the following supplies:

✔ first-aid supplies—different sizes of adhesive bandages, adhesive tape, gauze pads, antiseptic cream, scissors, tweezers, baby wipes, cotton pads, bottled water, syrup of ipecac, thermometer

✔ a list of the children in each vehicle

✔ medical emergency treatment forms for each child

✔ one operational, portable fire extinguisher for each car

Besides safety equipment, you may want to gather the following:

✔ drinking water and cups

✔ plastic bags for trash or dirty shoes and other clothing

✔ paper towels and antiseptic wipes or soap

✔ cordless mobile phone

✔ life jacket for each child for trips near water

✔ extra clothes for long trips with younger children

✔ ice chest for storing lunches for all-day field trips

✔ rain gear, hats, and sunscreen

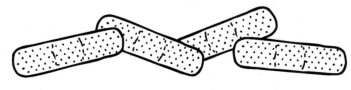

Notify Parents

You are required to give parents advance notice of field trips and to get their permission. At a minimum, you need to do the following preparations:

✔ Post a notice so parents will see it at least 48 hours before a field trip and keep it posted until the group returns. (A sample parent letter can be found on page 159.)

✔ The notice must list which groups of children are going, where they will go, and when they will leave and return. In some facilities, parents may not come in on a regular basis because friends or relatives drop off and pick up the children. If possible, publish your field trip plans in the school newsletter and/or calendar and send notes home to parents. Ask parents to bring any supplies their children may need, such as a hat, life jacket, and sunscreen, and include an invitation for parents to come along on the trip.

Transporting Children

If you are transporting the children in cars, each child must ride in a safety seat that is appropriate to the child's age, weight, and condition, with one seat belt per child and seat. A child may ride in a shoulder harness and seat belt if the harness goes across the child's chest and not across the face and neck. All adult drivers and passengers must be properly restrained when the vehicle is in motion. Children should not ride in the front seat if the car is equipped with a passenger side air bag.

Load and unload the children at the curbside of the vehicle or in a protected area. Always supervise children as they cross a street.

Traditional Field Trips

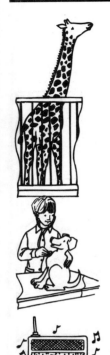

AIRPORT Small private airports make the best field trip. Ask to see the windsock, the runway, the airplanes, and hangers. Bring the children as close as possible to an airplane, and if possible, take them inside the cockpit or passenger area. Observe a plane landing or taking off.

AQUARIUM Ask for a guided, behind-the-scenes tour in addition to observing the tanks of fish.

BAKERY Ask for a tour through the kitchen. Look at equipment and flour storage areas, compare sizes of pans, see a cake decorating demonstration, and sample some goodies.

BANK Ask for a guided tour of the key areas of the bank. Observe how money is handled and where it is held for safekeeping.

BEACH For a great adventure, take a guide like a marine biologist. Comb and catch samples of marine life in nets and use books to identify catches-of-the-day.

BIRD WATCHING AREA Walk through a park, wildlife refuge, or other nature area. Ask a local Audubon Society to find an expert to act as a guide.

BOTANICAL GARDEN This field trip is best taken in spring or at harvest time so the children can observe planting or harvesting activities.

BUS STATION OR TRAIN STATION Schedule this field trip at a time when the station is not too busy. Tour the ticket area and continue through the waiting and loading areas.

CAR DEALERSHIP Visit a local car dealer. Ask to see new cars, used cars, the parts department, the waiting area, and the sales area. If possible, let the children sit in a brand new car.

CLOCK SHOP Visit a local shop. Study the various timepieces and listen to the sounds of the clocks and chimes.

CONSTRUCTION SITE Visit a local construction area. Ask for a guided tour. Talk about safety, clothing, equipment, and how a building is constructed. See close up the workings of a forklift, a back loader, a front loader, and other heavy equipment.

DAIRY This field trip requires an early morning start to see milking machines, barns, and equipment. Ask for a milking demonstration if you must go later.

DENTIST OFFICE Ask for a guided tour. Observe a teeth brushing demonstration.

FARM Traditional farms with a barn and farm animals make the best trip. Ask the farmer to show the children his or her equipment and feed.

FARM AND RANCH SHOP Look at farm equipment. Let the children compare their heights to those of tires. Ask to see a tractor do work.

FEED STORE Learn about tack, saddles, medicines, ropes, calf bottles, and feed at a local farm and ranch supply company.

FIRE DEPARTMENT Ask firefighters to give a fire safety talk and to show trucks, living quarters, maps, and equipment.

FLORIST Point out the cooler room, the live plants, and the gift arrangements. Ask the florist to demonstrate how to arrange flowers and make bows.

GROCERY STORE Ask for a tour that includes the freezer, the produce area storage, the meat market, the warehouse area, the bakery, and the business offices. Ask to observe any one-way mirrors.

HARDWARE STORE Watch how a key is made, compare sizes of nuts and bolts, and identify different tools.

HOSPITAL Ask if tours are available. See the emergency entrance, a laboratory, an X-ray machine, the maternity ward, and the gift shop.

INFANT SHOP Compare sizes of clothing, chairs, car seats, and other infant items.

KITE STORE Observe all the different kinds of kites. Ask for a kite demonstration.

LIBRARY Plan regular visits or schedule a one-time special event for a storytime session or an author talk.

LUMBERYARD Ask for an equipment demonstration and how to move and saw lumber.

MECHANIC SHOP Ask for a tour that allows the children to observe work through a window.

MUSIC STORE Compare sounds of instruments and look at unusual instruments.

NEIGHBORHOOD Take seasonal walks to observe changes in the environment. Teach about litter, water waste, and traffic safety.

NEWSPAPER OFFICE Visit the printing press and the editorial and advertising offices.

OPTOMETRIST Ask the optometrist to give a talk on eye care and safety.

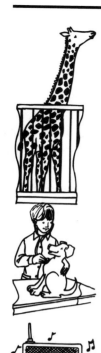

ORCHARD Go at blossom or harvest time to see the most activity.

PARK Draw pictures of the play area. Walk along the runner's path, observe animal life, study trees and other plants. Plan cooperative games and a picnic!

PET STORE Ask personnel to discuss the needs of pets and how to select them. Compare the different-sized pet homes. Point out pet medicine, grooming equipment, and cages.

PIZZA SHOP Ask for a tour that allows the children to make pizza.

PLANT NURSERY Look at plants native to the area, fruit trees, garden plants, evergreens, and water gardens. Ask the gardener to talk about the importance of plants and trees and to give tips on planting a children's garden.

POST OFFICE Ask the postal clerk to let the children follow a bright letter from the mail drop slot to the delivery truck.

POWER PLANT Check with your local electric or gas company to see if it offers tours. Ask the guide to talk about energy and its usefulness.

RECYCLING CENTER Ask for a talk and tour of the largest facility in your area because it will be recycling the most products.

SENIOR CITIZEN CENTER Plan a special visit with the activity director. Ask if the children can participate with the residents in cooperative activities—painting, coloring, reading, or planting.

SERVICE STATION Ask for a tour to watch a gasoline truck empty its tank or to safely observe a simple car repair and how to pump gasoline into a car.

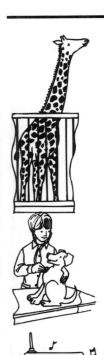

SHELL SHOP Point out different types of shells and talk about the marine life that inhabited them.

TELEPHONE COMPANY Talk to a repair person, discuss how telephones work, and look at equipment on a repair truck.

TELEVISION STATION Ask for the manager to demonstrate how a TV camera operates, visit the sound room, and tour where the news is broadcast. Ask if the children can work a camera.

UNIFORM SHOP Discuss the various uniforms worn by community helpers.

VETERINARY HOSPITAL Visit a small animal practice with grooming rooms or a farm animal practice. These are two very different field trips!

WATER TREATMENT PLANT Ask for a tour and talk on saving water. Talk about the importance of clean, healthy water.

WEATHER STATION Ask for a tour to see equipment used to study the weather and the observation room. Talk about different kinds of weather.

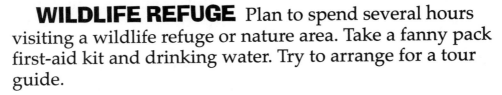

WILDLIFE REFUGE Plan to spend several hours visiting a wildlife refuge or nature area. Take a fanny pack first-aid kit and drinking water. Try to arrange for a tour guide.

X-RAY LAB Ask for a tour to see X-rays of different parts of the body and X-ray equipment.

YOGURT SHOP Take a tour and get free samples!

ZOO Ask if there are educational programs that complement what the children are studying. Ask if grants are available for admissions and programs.

Field Trip Alternatives

When a traditional field trip isn't practical, try planning backyard or playground field trips. These are wonderful experiences without the trials of transportation.

BEEKEEPERS Ask a beekeeper to show an empty hive and beekeeper clothing. Discuss safety around bees, and give out samples of honey.

BOAT OWNERS Ask a parent or owner of a boat shop to bring a boat the children can explore. Try getting a sailboat, a rubber raft, a canoe, and a motor boat all on the same day!

CLOWNS Invite professional party clowns to demonstrate how to put on make-up, dress in costumes, and perform tricks.

CONSERVATION SPECIALISTS Call a local environmental group and ask if a specialist will present a special children's program on litter, pollution, and soil conservation.

FARMERS Check in late winter when farmers are not so busy to see if they will bring a tractor, different kinds of seed, and other farm equipment. Ask if they will demonstrate how to prepare a spring garden area for your classroom, provided a tractor is allowed on the playground.

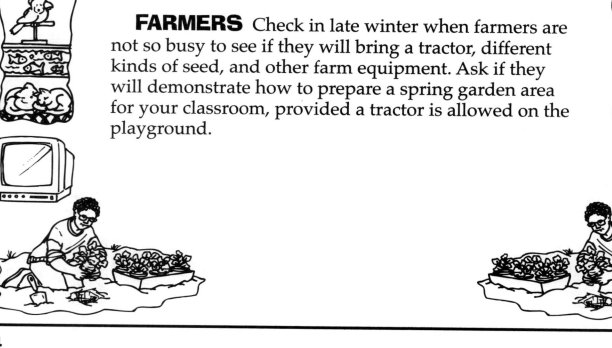

FIREFIGHTERS Ask if they will bring a truck, give a safety talk, and demonstrate how to use fire equipment.

GARDENERS Owners of garden shops and plant nurseries as well as home gardeners will often visit and share plants, seeds, and pictures. Ask if they will help plan and plant a garden for the children.

GEOLOGISTS Even jewelers and amateur rock hounds can provide wonderful specimens of rocks and beautiful books and posters.

LIFEGUARDS Many do programs on water safety.

MAIL CARRIERS Ask if they will let the children look inside postal trucks or cars.

MARINE BIOLOGISTS Ask if they will bring specimens to show in the classroom and explain the importance of keeping the beach and water clean. See if they will demonstrate how the food chain works.

MEDICAL PROFESSIONALS Nurses, doctors, dentists, and eye doctors will often present programs on health, safety, and other medical topics. Ask if they will wear their uniforms and bring medical tools and stories to share.

PARAMEDICS Find out if they will bring an ambulance for the children to explore, talk about medical emergencies, and reassure the children about hospitals.

PARENTS AND GRANDPARENTS Survey them about hobbies, travels, cultures, skills, and occupations. Invite them to share these things with the children.

PEST CONTROL PEOPLE Ask them to share insect collections and pictures. See if they will discuss helpful and harmful insects, poison safety, and equipment.

PET SHOP OWNERS Ask if they will talk about the importance of caring for pets, selecting the "right" pet, and the needs of pets.

PILOTS Private and commercial pilots can visit and talk about the basics of flying and airplane safety. They might be able to bring an ultra light plane for a demonstration on the playground. Hot-air balloonists will often demonstrate how a hot-air balloon works.

POLICE OFFICERS Ask if they will talk about safety and bring a patrol car that the children can explore.

RADIO AND TELEVISION PERSONALITIES
These favorites for children will often talk on the importance of being able to communicate.

SCUBA DIVERS Ask if they will dress in wet suits, demonstrate their equipment, and share slides or videos.

SHELL SHOP OWNERS They usually can bring a collection of shells and marine life to share.

TELEPHONE REPAIR PERSONNEL Ask if they will talk about the tools on their trucks and show how they climb poles.

VETERINARIANS Doctors and their assistants often visit and do programs on pets, safety, and health.

WEATHER FORECASTERS These favorites with children can talk about weather, weather symbols, forecasting, and storms.

ZOOS Ask if they have an outreach program to bring animals and programs to the school.

Aquarium

Take your children to a local aquarium. Try to get a behind-the-scenes tour of the facility. Ask if there are any marine species your little ones can touch or hold.

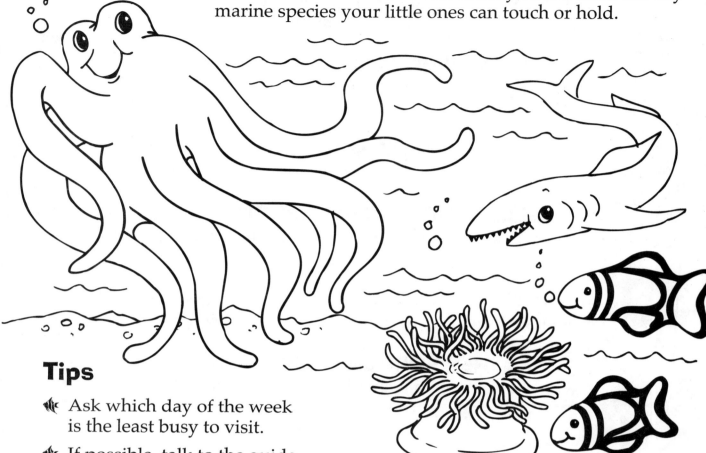

Tips

- Ask which day of the week is the least busy to visit.

- If possible, talk to the guide and explain what you want your children to experience.

- Ask for a group or educational discount.

- Establish limits and rules before entering the gift shop. (Some gift shops may not allow the whole group to enter at one time. Let part of the group eat a snack such as goldfish crackers while the rest of your children shop.)

Related Books

Aquarium Adventure, Peter Stadelmann, (Barron's Educational Series, 1998).

Aquarium Fish, Dick Mills, (D K Publishing, 1993).

Curious George Visits the Aquarium, Margret Rey, (Houghton Mifflin, 1984).

Fish Eyes: A Book You Can Count on, Lois Ehlert, (Harcourt Brace, 1992).

Fish Art

Let each child draw and paint his or her favorite fish. Attach each fish to a class thank-you card. Send the card to the staff at the aquarium.

Fish Feeding

Provide time for your children to observe goldfish feeding in a bowl. Point out the fins, gills, tail, and other details on the fish. Tell your children that fish breathe underwater using their gills. Ask your children how they think fish are like them and how fish are different from them.

Did You Ever See a Goldfish?

Sung to: "Did You Ever See a Lassie?"

Did you ever see a goldfish,
A goldfish, a goldfish?
Did you ever see a goldfish,
Go this way and that?

Go this way and that way,
And this way and that way,
Did you ever see a goldfish,
Go this way and that?

Marsha Elyn Wright

Aquarium

Marine Life Game

Make a memory game by cutting 20 squares of bright-colored posterboard. Buy a set of 10 pairs of matching marine life stickers. Place a marine life sticker on each square so you have 10 pairs of matching squares. Laminate the squares. Let your children play the memory match game in pairs or small groups.

Large to Small

Make a set of sequencing cards that show various sizes of fish from large to small. Let your children work together to order the cards from smallest to largest.

Sea Life Movement

Have your children pretend to be different kinds of ocean animals—octopus, starfish, fish, seal, whale, flying fish, sea turtle, eel. Ask them to show you how they would move in the ocean. Play music while they move. When the music stops, ask your children to pretend to be a different sea animal. Start the music again.

A Fishy Tale

Have your children help you write a tall tale about a fish that swims down a river and what silly, incredible things happen to that fish. Print the story on large mural paper. Let each child draw a fish on the mural paper to help illustrate your story.

Snacks

After visiting the aquarium, make different colors of gelatin. Let your children use fish-shaped cookie cutters to cut out fish shapes for a tasty snack. Place different types of fish-shaped crackers and fruit snacks in bowls for munching.

Bakery

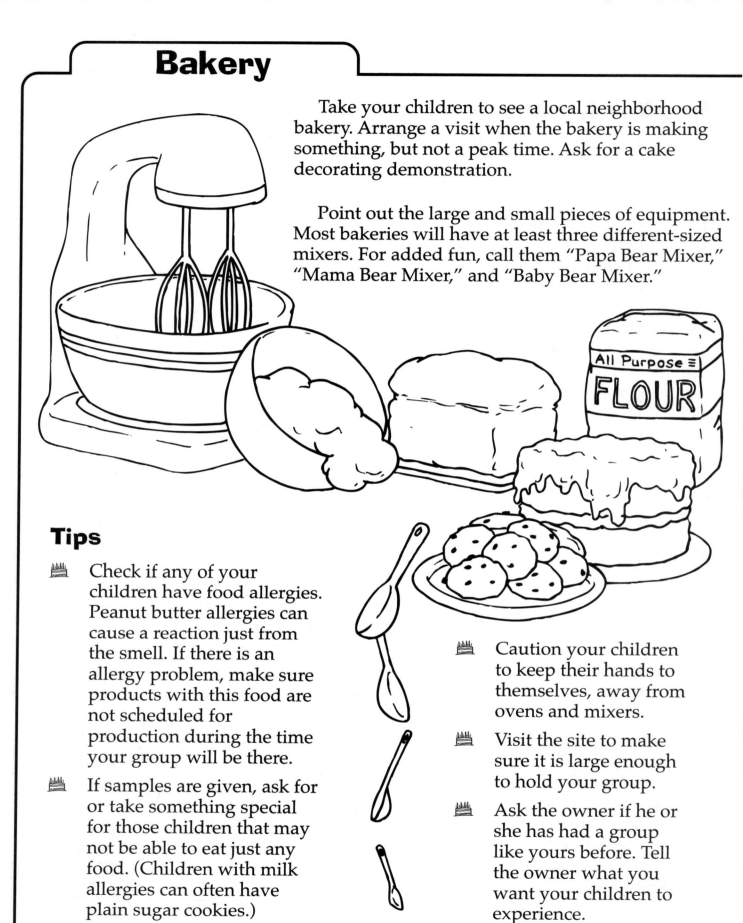

Take your children to see a local neighborhood bakery. Arrange a visit when the bakery is making something, but not a peak time. Ask for a cake decorating demonstration.

Point out the large and small pieces of equipment. Most bakeries will have at least three different-sized mixers. For added fun, call them "Papa Bear Mixer," "Mama Bear Mixer," and "Baby Bear Mixer."

All Purpose FLOUR

Tips

🎂 Check if any of your children have food allergies. Peanut butter allergies can cause a reaction just from the smell. If there is an allergy problem, make sure products with this food are not scheduled for production during the time your group will be there.

🎂 If samples are given, ask for or take something special for those children that may not be able to eat just any food. (Children with milk allergies can often have plain sugar cookies.)

🎂 Caution your children to keep their hands to themselves, away from ovens and mixers.

🎂 Visit the site to make sure it is large enough to hold your group.

🎂 Ask the owner if he or she has had a group like yours before. Tell the owner what you want your children to experience.

Large and Small

Collect a variety of clean, empty liquid containers such as a gallon, a half-gallon, a quart, and a pint. Introduce the vocabulary words *gallon, half-gallon, quart,* and *pint.* Explore with your children how much water each container holds. Let your children discover which container holds the most and which holds the least. Let the children place the containers from smallest to largest.

Related Books

Bread, Bread, Bread, Ann Morris, (William Morrow, 1993).

Hedgehog Bakes a Cake, Maryann MacDonald, (Bantam Books, 1991).

If You Give a Mouse a Cookie, Laura Joffe Numeroff, (HarperCollins, 1985).

In the Night Kitchen, Maurice Sendak, (HarperCollins, 1995).

Mix and Measure

Put cornmeal and flour in large bowls on a sand and water table. Add assorted mixing and measuring cups and spoons. Let your children pretend to be bakers as they mix and measure.

Bakery

The Muffin Man

Oh, do you know the muffin man,
The muffin man, the muffin man?
Oh, do you know the muffin man,
Who lives on Drury Lane?

Oh, yes, I know the muffin man,
The muffin man, the muffin man.
Oh, yes, I know the muffin man,
Who lives on Drury Lane.

Traditional

Scented Magnets

Help your children make cute, scented refrigerator magnets! Make a basic white bread and glue dough. Add a bit of ginger, cinnamon, and allspice to color the dough light brown. Use a cookie cutter to cut out gingerbread people shapes. Invite each child to decorate a gingerbread person. Set out bottles of glue, buttons, beads, rickrack, ribbon, and fabric scraps.

Allow the artwork to air dry several days. Attach a strip of magnetic tape to the back of each gingerbread person.

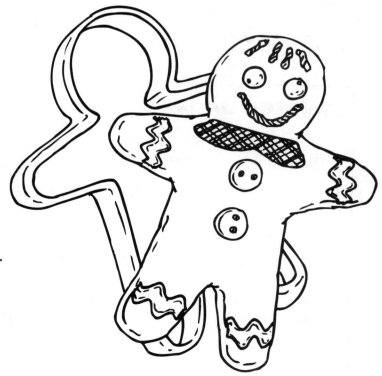

Sorting Game

Glue two business envelopes on the inside of a manila or construction paper folder. On one envelope, print "Things Found." On the other envelope, print "Things Not Found." On the front of the folder, print "Bakery."

Cut out magazine pictures of items normally found in a bakery and some items not found in a bakery. Place these cutouts inside a business envelope and staple it to the front of the folder. Provide time for your children to sort through the magazine pictures and place them inside the appropriate envelopes.

Cookie Bake

Have your children help you bake simple sugar cookies and decorate them with sprinkles. Talk about the changes that take place during the mixing and baking process. Send some of your cookies along with a class thank-you letter to the bakery.

Bank

Take your children to see a local branch bank or savings and loan office. Arrange a visit when the bank is not too busy. Ask for a behind-the-scenes tour so your children can see a vault, computers, teller computers, video cameras, etc. See if the bank manager will talk about the difference between savings and loans, how money is made, and where money is stored after it leaves the bank.

Tips

- Caution your children to keep their hands to themselves, away from computers and other bank equipment.

- Ask the branch manager if he or she has had a group like yours before. Tell the manager what you want your children to experience.

- Remind your children to walk quietly inside the bank so as not to disturb workers and customers.

Related Books

The Big Green Pocketbook, Candice Ransom, (HarperCollins, 1993).

Corduroy, Don Freeman, (Viking, 1968).

Money, Money, Money, Nancy Winslow Parker, (HarperCollins, 1995).

Shop Talk

Set up a shop in your classroom. Display items that are safe to play with for three-year-olds (small toys, wooden spoons, plastic cups, etc.). Attach a blank paper price tag on each item. Reproduce the play money on page 29. Cut out the money and glue one cutout to each tag.

Reproduce several copies of the play money on page 29. Laminate the pages and cut out the money. Give each child a dollar bill of play money and one of each paper coin. Allow small groups to "go shopping." Let your children take turns being shop clerks. After a group is done shopping, let the children share with the class which items they bought. Then have the shoppers return the items to the store and get back their play money.

Coin Banks

Collect small containers with reclosable lids such as nonclorine bleach and detergent boxes or cocoa containers. Cut slots in the lids to make coin banks.

Give one bank to each child. Gather a variety of stickers and cut out simple shapes from construction paper and self-stick paper. Let the children attach stickers and self-stick shapes and glue colorful paper shapes on the banks to decorate them. Give each child a penny to drop into the slot!

Coin, Coin, Who's Got the Coin?

Have your children sit in a circle. Show them a quarter in play money. Choose one child to sit in the middle of the circle. Tell the children that while the music plays, they are to pass the quarter around the circle while the center child has his or her eyes closed. When the music stops, the center child gets three chances to guess who is holding the coin. Watch out for giggles! Choose a new child to guess each time you start a new game.

M-O-N-E-Y

Sung to: "Bingo"

A penny, nickel, quarter, dime,
And dollar bill to save-O!
M-O-N-E-Y, M-O-N-E-Y, M-O-N-E-Y,
This money can I save-O!

Marsha Elyn Wright

Cookie Coins

Make batter for simple sugar cookies and chill the dough. Then roll it out flat. Let the children use round cookie cutters to cut out coin shapes. Bake the cookies. After the cookies cool, give each child a cookie.

Let the children use frosting to print a "1" on the cookies to represent pennies. For an added touch, print a "¢" sign beside each child's printed "1." Eat and enjoy!

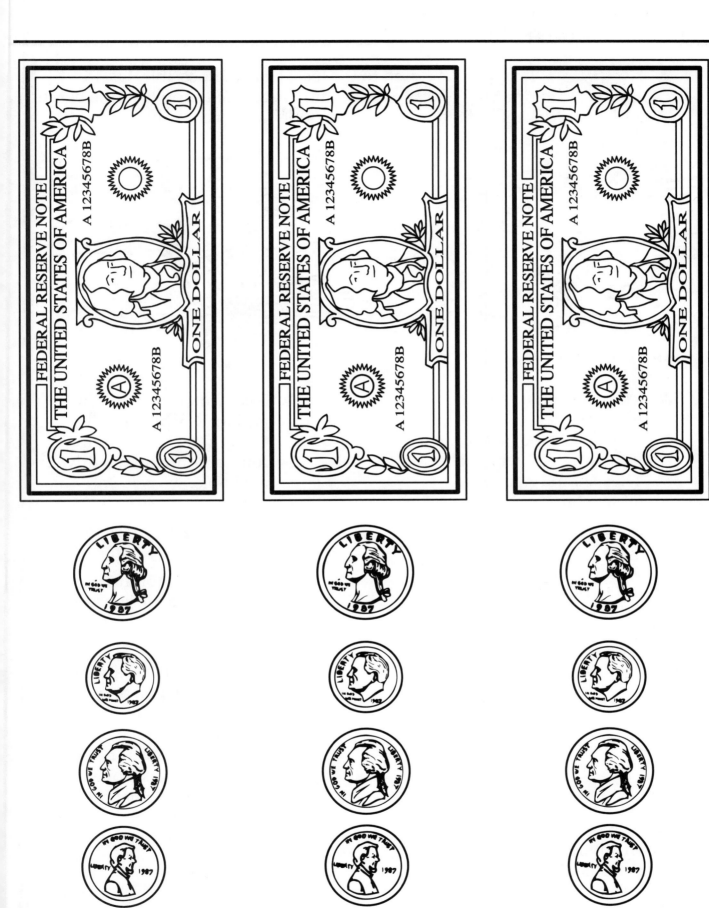

Beach

Take your children to the local beach. If possible, take a marine biologist as a guide and visit a shell shop near the beach. Make it a full day trip that includes a picnic lunch!

Tips

⛵ Make sure your children wear life jackets any time they are on the beach, even if the water is very shallow. They should not be allowed in the water.

⛵ Make sure each child has a collection jug (plastic milk or juice jug with part of the top removed). Print each child's name on a jug. Let the children use their jugs for beach combing and collecting.

⛵ Make sure the children wear sturdy shoes and clothing to protect them from the sun. Ask the parents to apply sunscreen before they leave for school to avoid liability if there is an allergic reaction.

⛵ Take water for drinking and for washing hands. Bathrooms and drinking fountains are not readily available.

⛵ Take tubs or plastic bags for storing sandy shoes during the trip home.

⛵ Take plastic goldfish bowls or plastic jars to put specimens in for observation.

⛵ If possible, invite a marine biologist or a parent who is familiar with marine life to be your guide. Ask if he or she would catch some marine life in a net for the children to observe, and then release.

Sorting Shells

Display a variety of seashells for the children to observe. Place four large paper circles, each a different color, near the shells. Ask your children to sort the shells into two, three, or four groups by placing shells that are alike in some way on the same color circles. Talk about color, shape, size, texture, and weight.

Crab Walk

Let the children move sideways like crabs. Line up the children in rows and tell them where to crab walk, not too far! They move sideways "walking" on their hands and feet, keeping their bottoms up!

Related Books

At the Beach, Ann F. Rockwell, (Simon & Schuster, 1991).

A House for Hermit Crab, Eric Carle, (Simon & Schuster, 1990).

On My Beach There Are Many Pebbles, Leo Lionni, (William Morrow, 1994).

Serpent Shell, David Ross, (Demco Media, 1993).

Beach

Sea Scape Collage

Supply your children with sand and small seashells. Encourage them to create a model of the beach on a piece of blue posterboard.

Let the children sprinkle the sand and place seashells on their landscapes to make the beaches.

Parent Litter Patrol

While at the beach, collect clean trash. At school, display the litter. Talk about each item and how it harms the environment and the wildlife. Discuss how to help keep beaches free from litter.

Movement Fun

Let five children at a time pretend to be sea life swimming in the sea. (Or, start the game with any number of children.) As you recite the following rhyme, signal one "creature" at a time to jump out of the sea.

Five tiny creatures,
Swimming in the sea,
One jumped out,
And wiggled with glee!

Four tiny creatures,
Swimming in the sea,
One jumped out,
And wiggled with glee!

Three tiny creatures,
Swimming in the sea,
One jumped out,
And wiggled with glee!

Two tiny creatures,
Swimming in the sea,
One jumped out,
And wiggled with glee!

One tiny creature,
Swimming in the sea,
It jumped out,
And wiggled with glee!

No tiny creatures,
Swimming in the sea,
They crawled on the sand,
And wiggled with glee!

Ha! Ha! Ha! Ha! Ha!

Marsha Elyn Wright

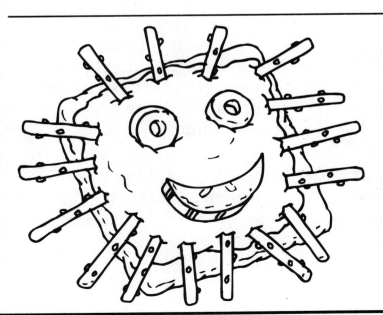

Silly Sea Life Snacks

Let your children spread softened cream cheese on crackers. Then let them choose shredded cheese, sliced olives, and other toppings to sprinkle on top of the crackers to make silly sea life creatures. Encourage the children to make up names for their sea life. Eat and enjoy!

Bird Watching Area

Take the children to a local park, wildlife refuge, or other nature area. Your children will enjoy seeing and hearing the birds. They will also enjoy seeing bird tracks, nests, and feeding areas. If you are lucky, you may find some feathers. (Leave the feathers in the area unless you have special permission to remove them. It may be against the law to possess the feather.) Be careful not to disturb any nests or tracks.

Tips

🐦 Schedule the trip during the time of the year that will have the largest population of birds.

🐦 Do a practice walk around the school, stressing the importance of walking and sitting quietly.

🐦 If it is a wooded area, make sure each child wears long pants, socks, and shoes. Put pant legs inside the socks and spray the socks with an insect repellent that is safe for children. (Ask the child's parents to do the spraying to avoid liability in case of a reaction.)

🐦 Invite someone who is familiar with the birds in that area to act as a guide. Ask if he or she has books about birds to share with the children.

Bird Feeders

Make simple bird feeders to hang around the school. Collect several cardboard tubes from paper toweling or toilet paper rolls. Punch two holes in the top of each cardboard tube and attach a length of string or thin wire for hanging.

Pour honey in empty pie tins and birdseed in plastic bowls. Let the children lightly roll the cardboard tubes in the honey and then sprinkle birdseed on the tubes. Have wet paper towels on hand for washing sticky fingers!

Help the children hang the bird feeders in trees around the school.

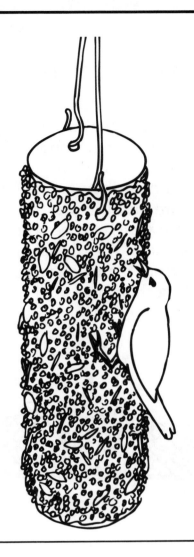

Related Books

Bird Nests, Barrie Watts, (Silver Burdett Press, 1990).

Have You Seen Birds?, Joanne R. Oppenheim, (Scholastic, 1990).

Heron Street, Ann Warren Turner, (HarperCollins Children's, 1989).

Bird Watching Area

Help Birds Build Nests

Wrap a piece of plastic mesh over a clothes hanger and loosely pull lengths of string, ribbon, cotton balls, and fabric through the holes. Hang the mesh in an area where birds are building nests. Let your children watch to see if any birds pull some of the ribbon and other items from the mesh to use in building their nests.

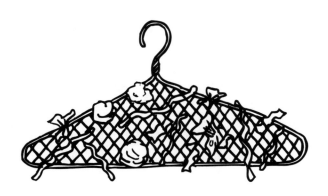

Sequencing Cards

Make sequencing cards by finding magazine pictures of the following: bird building a nest, nest with one egg, nest with several eggs, birds sitting on a nest, nest with baby birds hatching, baby birds that have growing feathers, baby birds beginning to fly, and an empty nest. Glue each picture to a piece of construction paper. Display the cards on a bulletin board. Talk about the pictures. Help the children sequence the cards.

Bird Puppet Pals

Cut out red, blue, and yellow bird shapes from sturdy construction paper. Let the children glue on button eyes and feathers. Glue a craft stick to the back of each bird. Allow time for each child to share his or her bird puppet pal with the class. Let the children name their pals. Encourage each child to each tell a story about his or her bird.

Two Little Bluebirds

(Finger Play)

Two little bluebirds,
Sitting on a hill. *(pointer fingers up)*

One named Jack. *(one hand forward)*
One named Jill. *(other hand forward)*

Fly away Jack. *(one hand behind back)*
Fly away Jill. *(other hand behind back)*

Come back, Jack. *(one hand forward)*
Come back, Jill. *(other hand forward)*

Traditional

Deviled Egg Snacks

Make deviled eggs for a snack! Place eggs that are room temperature in a pan of boiling water. Make sure the water covers the eggs. Reduce the temperature so the water just simmers. Cook 15 to 20 minutes.

Crack the cooked eggs. Then plunge them immediately into cold water. (This helps prevent the yolk from darkening.) Shell the eggs and cut in half. Scoop out the yolks and mash them with some mayonnaise. Add a bit of salt and pepper. If you want, add a teaspoon of grated cheese for each egg. Fill the whites with the seasoned yolks.

Botanical Garden

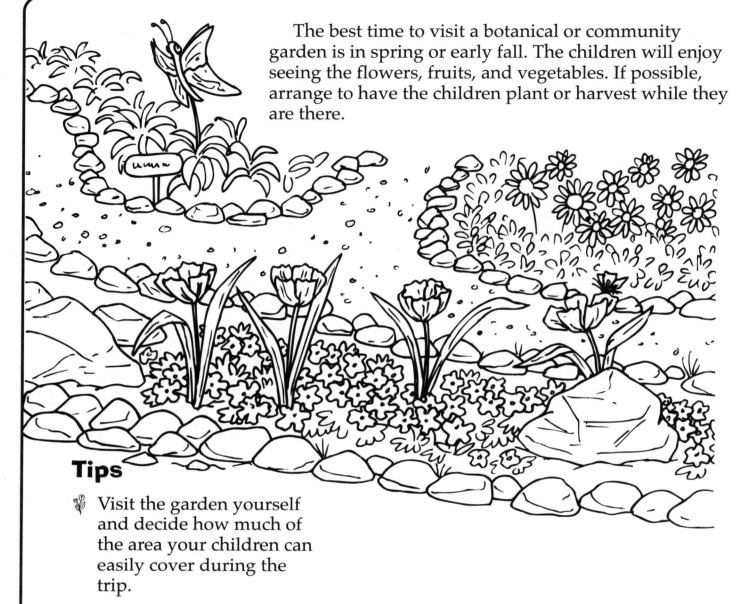

The best time to visit a botanical or community garden is in spring or early fall. The children will enjoy seeing the flowers, fruits, and vegetables. If possible, arrange to have the children plant or harvest while they are there.

Tips

❧ Visit the garden yourself and decide how much of the area your children can easily cover during the trip.

❧ Make sure the children wear proper shoes for walking on the paths. Discourage the children from wearing sandals. Tiny feet in sandals can get injured walking on the gravel paths.

❧ Ask to see the compost areas, the potting shed, and other important areas.

❧ Warn the children that insects are a part of garden life. Tell the children to look carefully before they smell the flowers.

❧ Check to see if any of the children are allergic to insect bites.

❧ Take insect sting medication in case of an insect bite.

Ten in a Row

Sung to: "Ten in a Bed"

There were ten in the row,
And the gardener said,
"I'll pick one. I'll pick one."
So snip went the clippers,
And one was gone . . .

There were nine in the row,
And the gardener said,
"I'll pick one. I'll pick one."
So snip went the clippers,
And one was gone . . .

(Continue the song by counting
one less with each repetition until
the last verse below.)

There was one in the row,
And the gardener said,
"I'll pick one. I'll pick one."
So snip went the clippers,
Now it's time to plant!

Marsha Elyn Wright

Have 10 children pretend to be
flowers, fruits, or vegetables and
stand in a row. You can pretend to
be the gardener and "snip" one
child from the garden each time.
You can also tell the story using a
flannelboard with felt flowers,
fruits, or vegetables to help the
children visualize the story.

Torn Paper Creations

Display pictures of a variety of
flowers and fruits. Talk with the
children about the different colors,
shapes, and sizes they see. Let the
children tear scraps of assorted
paper and glue them onto precut
flower or fruit shapes. Have them
mount these torn creations on a
sheet of sturdy paper.

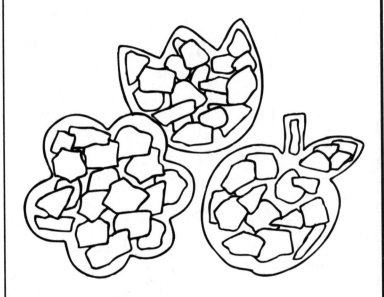

Related Books

The Carrot Seed, Ruth Krauss,
(HarperCollins, 1993).

*Keeper of Life: Discovering Plants
Through Native American Stories and
Earth Activities*, Joseph Bruchac,
(Fulcrum Publishing, 1997).

Planting a Rainbow, Lois Ehlert,
(Harcourt Brace, 1992).

Stories for All Seasons (The Tiny Seed),
Eric Carle, (Simon & Schuster,
1998).

Botanical Garden

Flower Movement

Take your children outdoors. Tell them to pretend they are tiny seeds and that you are going to "plant" them in the soil. Position the children in different spots on the grass and tell them to crouch down as if they are seeds. At your signal, have the children very slowly wiggle about and stand up as if they are flowers growing!

Pop Up Flowers

Cut various sizes of circles and petals out of different colors of paper. Have each child glue some petals around a circle to make a flower. Let the children add stems by gluing their flowers to craft sticks and coloring their stems green.

Cut several 1" x 3" strips of green paper. Give each child a paper cup. Have the children glue green strips on the outside of the cups to make grass. Poke a hole in the bottom of each cup. Let the children poke their stems through the hole going from the inside of the cup.

Watch the flowers grow! Have each child hold the stem on the end that's poking through the bottom of the cup and push it up above the cup to make the flower "grow."

Flower Snacks

Cut various fruits into circles. Arrange pears and peaches around each circle to create flower snacks. Add raisins on the blossoms and zucchini stick stems. Let the children enjoy these flower snacks while you read a garden story.

Sprouting Seeds

Give each child a resealable plastic bag. Have the children moisten cotton balls or white paper toweling with water. Let the children "plant" some seeds in their bags. Watch the seeds in the bag sprout! After sprouting, let the children plant their seedlings in the soil for a classroom garden.

Three Little Seeds

Sung to: "Three Blind Mice"

Three small seeds,
Three small seeds,
All in a row,
All in a row,
They grew so tall in the warm sunlight,
They spread out their petals with colors bright,
Their leaves were so green, oh, what a sight,
Those three small seeds!

Marsha Elyn Wright

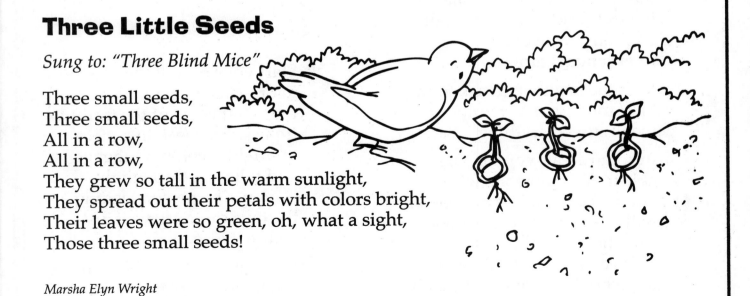

Bus Station, Train Station, or Airport

It may be possible to visit more than one transportation facility in a day, depending on the locations and travel time required. This kind of a field trip provides a wonderful opportunity to compare the work that takes place at different locations.

Tips

✈ When possible, choose the smallest facility available. For example, choose a small local airport over an international airport.

✈ Visit the facility and ask for a brief tour. Look carefully to make sure everything is safe.

✈ In some areas, you may be able to find someone with a hot-air balloon. The balloonist will often inflate the balloon and show it to the children. This can usually be done on the schoolyard or at a local air strip.

✈ Start your tour at the check-in or ticket area and work though the rest of the facility. If possible, check in a piece of brightly colored luggage and follow it through the station. The person leading the tour can retrieve it just before it is loaded.

✈ If possible, let the children briefly tour a plane, train, or bus.

Related Books

A Busy Day at the Airport, Philippe Dupasquier, (Candlewick Press, 1995).

A Busy Day at the Train Station, Philippe Dupasquier, (Candlewick Press, 1996).

Jonathan Goes to the Airport, Susan K. Baggette, (Brookfield, 1998).

Mabel Takes the Ferry, Emily Chetkowski, (Herit Publishing, 1995).

School Bus, Donald Crews, (William Morrow, 1993).

Train Leaves the Station, Eve Merriam, (Henry Holt, 1994).

Wheels on the Bus, Raffi, (Crown Books, 1998).

The Yellow Boat, Margaret Hilbert, (Modern Curriculum, 1989).

Land, Air, and Water

Cut out of construction paper a large, white, puffy cloud, a large blue lake, and a long strip of brown land. Then cut out magazine pictures of different modes of travel—helicopter, airplane, sailboat, motorcycle, jet, hot-air balloon, ship, etc.

Have the children do a sorting activity. Tell them to place on the cloud the pictures of things that fly in the air. They can place on the lake pictures of things that travel in water. They can place on the land pictures of things that travel on land.

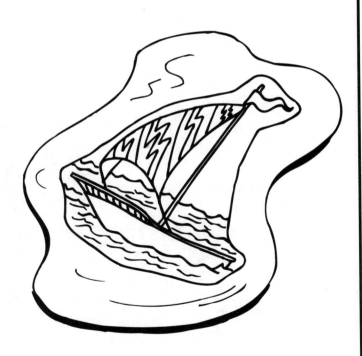

Bus Station, Train Station, or Airport

Let's Travel!

Set up chairs and boxes to make big pretend vehicles. Place in a box different kinds of hats that pilots, captains, and train conductors might wear. Have nearby some small luggage, empty plastic bottles, and play cameras. Let the children get ready for a pretend trip by packing and unpacking the suitcases. Let them take turns boarding and unloading the vehicles.

Zoom!

Place different types of transportation toys in the sand table and in the block area. Let the children explore and play with all kinds of transportation.

Talk with the children about the different sounds the vehicles make. Let the children create sounds for each type of travel—zoom, roar, zip, etc.

Paper Transportation

Collect crayons, buttons, pipe cleaners, small, different-sized boxes, and sheets of paper. Help the children make and decorate paper airplanes. Help the children make cars, trucks, and trains out of the boxes. Poke holes in the vehicles and let the children use pipe cleaners to attach button wheels to their vehicles.

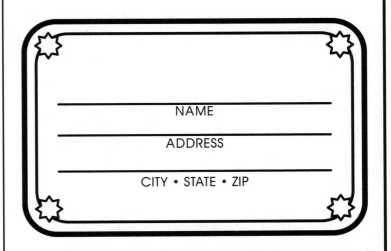

Luggage Tags

Let each child design a luggage tag that contains his or her name and address. Help the children print the information. Laminate each tag and attach it to their backpacks or lunch totes.

Airplane Snacks

Provide trays for each child. Place chairs in rows of two with an aisle down the middle. Let different children play the role of the pilots and flight attendants. Let the rest of the children board the airplane, take a seat, and prepare to eat.

Place a small snack of pretzels and a plastic cup of fruit punch on each tray. Serve the passengers. Have helper attendants pass around wet paper towels for cleaning hands.

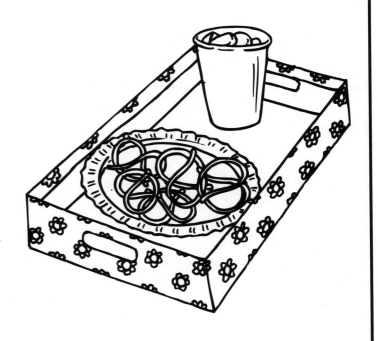

Clock Shop

Exploring a clock shop can be a magical learning experience for young children. Choose a shop that has a large variety of clocks in all shapes and sizes. Let your children hear the sounds the clocks make and stay long enough to hear the hour chimes.

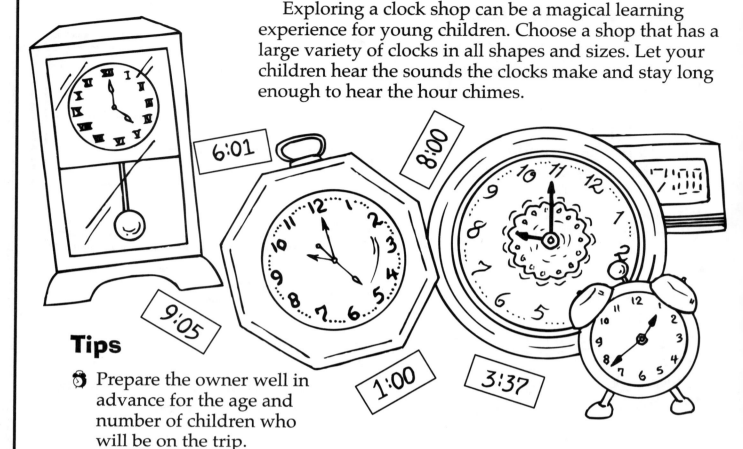

Tips

⏰ Prepare the owner well in advance for the age and number of children who will be on the trip.

⏰ Make sure the shop is large enough for the group to move about easily.

⏰ Remind the children to keep their hands in their pockets or to themselves.

⏰ Make this rule: Do not touch unless permission is given.

⏰ Plan this trip when heavy coats will not be needed. Most shops will not have a place for coats when they are removed.

Related Books

The Clock Book: Learn to Tell Time, Kate Mason, (Troll, 1996).

Clocks and More Clocks, Pat Hutchins, (Macmillan, 1970).

My First Clock, Playskool Books, (Dutton, 1997).

The Real Mother Goose Clock Book, Jane Chambless-Rigie, (Scholastic, 1997).

Tick Tock Clock, Sharon Gordon, (Troll, 1992).

Tick Tock Tales: Stories to Read About the Clock, Margaret Mahy, (Simon & Schuster, 1994).

Classroom Clock Collage

Let the children make a clock collage for the classroom. Have a variety of rubber stamps the children can use to print assorted sizes of clocks. If possible, cut out magazine pictures of different types of clocks.

Give the children time to stamp clock faces and glue clock cutouts on a large circle of construction paper.

Keeping Time

Give each child a set of rhythm sticks, wood blocks, or egg shakers. Let the children tap out the ticking of a clock as you sing "Hickory Dickory Dock." Give some children triangles to use to sound the chimes when the clock strikes the hour!

Clock Works

Set out a variety of clocks and watches. Ask parents to bring minute timers, sundials, wind-up clocks, and other clocks to share. Talk to the children about the different power sources for the clocks. Take the children outside on a sunny day to show them how a sundial works. Show the children how to set a clock. Talk about safety when using electricity and batteries. Then let the children play with the clocks.

Clock Shop

Paper Plate Clocks

Make a clock face circle that fits in the center of a large paper plate, one for each child. Print the clock face numbers large and bold. Make a set of sturdy paper clock hands for each clock face.

Have each child glue a clock face on the middle of a large paper plate. Help each child poke a brad through the end of a set of clock hands and attach it through the middle of his or her clock face. Then let them add colorful crayon designs to personalize their clocks.

Let the children examine the hands of a real clock. Let the children move their clock hands around the clock to understand a clockwise direction.

Clock Hands Moving

Have your children pretend to be alarm clocks. Ask them to move their arms like the hands on a clock. Use a set of rhythm sticks to tap out the ticking of a clock. Let the children sway left and right to keep time. Have the children straighten their arms and move them in a clockwise direction beginning at the head and moving clockwise around their bodies until they reach the head again. Let them each sound an alarm on the hour!

Around the Clock Book

Make a class big book that shows what children do at different times of the day. Draw a clock face that shows 8:00. Ask the children what they are doing around that time in the morning. Draw a clock face that shows 12:00. Ask the children what they are usually doing at that time of the day. Draw two more different clock times and talk about the activities done at those times.

Give each child one large sheet of construction paper. Ask them to draw a clock face showing one of the four times you discussed. Help the children form the numbers for their clocks. Have the children draw pictures of themselves doing activities for the times shown on their clocks.

Assemble the pages into a class book about time. Title your book "Around the Clock." Let the children take turns sharing the book with their families.

Rice Cake Clocks

Let the children spread peanut butter on rice cakes. Place raisins around the edges of the peanut butter to represent numerals on a clock. Let the children place carrot sticks on the clocks to represent the hands of a clock. If you wish, have the children position the carrot clock hands at one o'clock. When it's really one o'clock, eat these delicious clock snacks!

Construction Site

If there is a local construction site within walking distance, you can make periodic visits to observe the progress. This is a wonderful experience for young children to learn how machines work.

Tips

- Prepare the general contractor in advance for the age and number of children who will be visiting the site.

- Ask if there is a preferred day the children should visit so they can see a foundation poured, to see roof beams and rafters being raised, etc.

- Ask if there are safety restrictions or rules that the children must follow.

- Ask if the children will wear hard hats or other safety equipment.

- Remind the children to stay away from moving vehicles and keep a safe distance from the actual building under construction.

- Ask the general contractor to show the children specific machines and tell how they work.

Construction Corner

Place bulldozers, trucks, dump trucks, and other construction toys as well as a variety of wooden blocks in one area of the sandbox or sand table. Let the children construct their own buildings!

Toy Houses

Give each child a sheet of drawing paper and have him or her draw a simple house. Ask the children to construct their homes using blocks, Lincoln Logs™, Tinker Toys™, and Duplo™ building sets.

Give the children time to share their drawings and buildings with one another.

Related Books

Block City, Robert Louis Stevenson, (Dutton, 1988).

Building a House, Byron Barton, (Greenwillow, 1981).

Changes, Changes, Pat Hutchins, (Macmillan, 1971).

Dig, Fill, Dump, Fill, Tana Hoban, (Greenwillow, 1975).

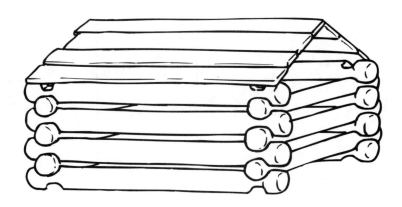

A Class Book

Talk with your children about some of the things used to build houses—bricks, lumber, plaster, steel, etc. Talk about what things would be fun to use to build an imaginary house.

Then make a class book entitled "This Is the House That I Built." At the bottom of a sheet of drawing paper, print "I built my house out of _____." Copy a class set and give one page to each child.

Help each child finish the sentence. Have the children illustrate their sentences and draw themselves as construction workers. Bind the pages into a class book.

Painting Fun

Collect large empty boxes. Let the children create a box city on the play area. Ask parents to help cut doors and windows. Let the children paint their buildings with water-based paints.

For added fun, let the children use water, paint rollers, and pans to "water" paint a school play house or an outside wall.

I'm a Little Builder

Sung to: "I'm a Little Teapot"

I'm a little builder,
Strong and tall,
I pound my hammer,
And build a wall,
When my work is over,
I can rest.
I smile because I did my best!

Marsha Elyn Wright

Three Little Pigs

Read the story "The Three Little Pigs." Let the children take turns acting out the story while you narrate it. Set up props: dried grass for straw in a small box, sticks for twigs in another box, and blocks for bricks in a third box. Let these be the peddlers' carts.

Make cute paper pig noses out of pink paper circles and attach them with loops of tape. Attach brown construction paper wolf ears on a paper headband for the wolf's costume.

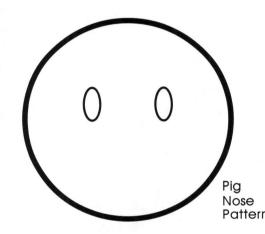

Pig Nose Pattern

Construction Site Snacks

Have the children use graham crackers and peanut butter to construct tiny buildings they can eat. Show them how to use the crackers and peanut butter like bricks and mortar. Let the children share their constructions before eating them!

Dairy

Excitement will build and smiles will spread when you take your children to a dairy farm! They will love the animals and be amazed by the sights, sounds, and smells.

Tips

🐄 Milking is done very early in the morning or late in the afternoon. If you cannot go during these hours to observe milking firsthand, ask for a demonstration.

🐄 Have the children wear old shoes. Take plastic bags for carrying dirty shoes.

🐄 Prepare the children in advance for the different barnyard smells and sounds.

🐄 Dairies usually have the biggest numbers of young calves in the late winter or early spring. Try to schedule your trip during this time.

🐄 Check ahead of time with the farmer about the best time to visit.

Related Books

Duke the Dairy Delight Dog, Lisa Campbell Ernst, (Simon & Schuster, 1996).

Hooray for Dairy Farming!, Bobbie Kalman, (Crabtree Publishing, 1997).

Heartland, Diane Siebert, (HarperCollins Children's, 1992).

Milk Makers, Gail Gibbons, (Simon & Schuster, 1996).

Making Butter

Fill baby food jars half full of whipping cream and screw the lids on tightly. Assign each child a partner and give each pair of children a baby food jar of whipping cream. Tell the children to take turns shaking the jars. Tell the children to watch how the whipping cream changes form. After about six minutes, the cream will be whipped, and a few minutes later, the cream will form yellow balls of butter!

Pour out the liquid whey. Fill each jar about three times with cold water and drain off to wash the butter. Add a little salt, then spread the butter on crackers and enjoy!

Pudding Paint

Let your children help you mix milk with vanilla instant pudding. Place thickened pudding in small plastic containers and add a variety of food coloring to create different colors of pudding paint.

Cover your art area with newspaper. Have your children wash their hands. Give each child fingerpaint paper. Let the children fingerpaint with the pudding colors to paint a picture of a farm animal. Your children will enjoy creating these yummy animals!

Dairy

Painting With Milk

Pour small amounts of evaporated milk in muffin tins. Add two or three drops of different colors of food coloring to the milk and stir. Let the children paint pictures of dairy cows on sturdy sheets of construction paper.

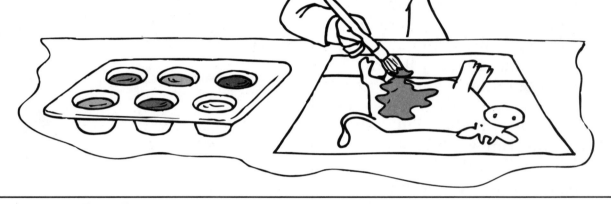

Milking Fun

Set up a pretend cow and let the children practice milking by hand. Make a heavy cardboard cutout of a cow and attach it to the side of a table, a children's ironing board, or a short saw horse. Use a latex glove for the udder. Put a small hole in each of the fingers and fill the glove with water or water with some white tempera paint. Provide a small stool and a bucket.

Math Match-Up

Cut out 20 paper squares. Print a different number from 1 to 10 on 10 of the squares. On another square, draw one cow, on another square, draw two cows, on a third square, draw three cows, and so on, until you have a set of squares showing groups of cows 1 to 10.

Let the children match the number(s) with the correct number of cows.

Milk, Oh, Wow!

Sung to: "Row, Row, Row Your Boat"

Milk, milk, milk, oh, wow!
Ice cream, cottage cheese,
Yogurt and
    whipped cream and
    butter and
    cream cheese, oh,
Thank you, Mrs. Cow!

Marsha Elyn Wright

Snack Time

Mix ¼ cup plain yogurt, ¾ cup sour cream, and one package of dry vegetable soup mix by hand in a bowl. (Add more sour cream if needed for milder taste.) Refrigerate ½ hour. Serve with crackers, carrot and celery sticks, and zucchini slices.

Dentist Office

This trip can be an important one, especially if your children have not visited the dentist yet with their parents. A good children's dentist can calm fears and can stress good oral hygiene.

Tips

- Make sure the dentist has experience working with and talking to younger children.

- Take extra help in case some of the children have had a bad experience and are nervous about visiting a dentist's office.

- Ask for free toothbrushes and toothpaste.

- Make sure the dentist and staff demonstrate how they will look dressed with their face mask, gloves, and protective clothing. Have the person dress in front of the children.

- If this trip isn't possible, ask a dentist to visit your classroom.

Related Books

Doctor deSoto, William Steig, (Farrar, Straus, and Giroux, 1982).

Going to the Dentist, Helen Frost, (Children's Press, 1998).

Just Going to the Dentist, Mercer Mayer, (Golden Books, 1990).

Little Rabbit's Loose Tooth, Lucy Bates, (Crown Books, 1983).

My First Dentist Visit, Julia Allen, (A R O Publishing, 1987).

My Visit to the Dentist, Pam Howard, (HighReach, 1995).

Practice Brushing

Have a set of practice plastic teeth and a toothbrush available at school for the children to practice brushing their teeth. You may be able to borrow these from the dentist. You can also purchase a set. Teeth-shaped ice tongs will work and can sometimes be found in gag gift shops.

Brushing Charts

Make a tooth-brushing chart for each child to take home and record how many times he or she brushes in one week.

Tooth Fairy Pillows

Discuss how losing baby teeth is natural and normal for children. Make a tooth fairy box or pillow for each child to take home. Cut pairs of simple tooth shapes out of white felt. Stitch or glue the sides and bottom of the felt pieces together. Glue on wiggly eyes, a pompon nose, and a red felt smile. Stuff the pillow with a cotton ball.

Fancy envelopes also work well as "tooth fairy pillows." Let the children decorate the envelopes with markers, stickers, and stamps.

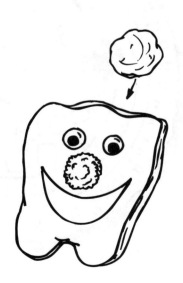

Dentist Office

What Germs Can Do!

Put a chicken bone or raw egg in a cup of vinegar. Let it sit a few days. Tell your children that the vinegar represents the acid that germs in their mouths create and the bone (or egg) represents their teeth.

After several days, let the children observe how the bone has become soft and bendable. Stress to the children that brushing their teeth helps remove the germs that can soften teeth.

Toothy Grins

Give each child a large paper plate, a large red paper smile, and a ½-inch wide, white paper strip. Have the children glue the smiles on the paper plates to make smiling faces. Then have each child cut the white paper strip into small pieces to make teeth. Tell the children to glue the teeth on their smiles. Let the children finish the faces by drawing eyes, noses, and other facial details. Display the toothy grins on a bulletin board and talk with the children about how they can have beautiful toothy grins!

Sorting Treats and Snacks

Cut out magazine pictures of high-sugar treats (candy and cookies) and low-sugar snacks (crackers and cheese, pretzels, bagels, carrots, popcorn). Display them for your children to see. Talk with your children about the different sweet treats and the low-sugar snacks. Tell them that to keep teeth happy and healthy, they should eat more snacks than sweets.

Cut white paper into large, simple tooth shapes and give each child a pair of teeth. Have each child draw a happy face on one tooth and a sad face on the other tooth. Let the children sort through the magazine pictures and choose a treat and a snack. Have the children glue the treat on the sad face and the snack on the happy face.

Crunchy Snacks

Tell your children that apples, carrots, and other fruit and vegetable snacks keep teeth "happy and healthy." Cut up a variety of fruits and vegetables and let the children crunch away!

Toothpaste on the Brush

Sung to: "Wheels on the Bus"

Toothpaste on the brush
Goes round and round,
Round and round,
Round and round.
Toothpaste on the brush,
Goes round and round.
I scrub the germs away!

Marsha Elyn Wright

Farm

Try to take your children to a traditional farm with animals and crops. Spring or fall is usually the best time to plan this trip. The children will enjoy seeing baby animals born in the spring. Ask if the children could take part in feeding some of the animals.

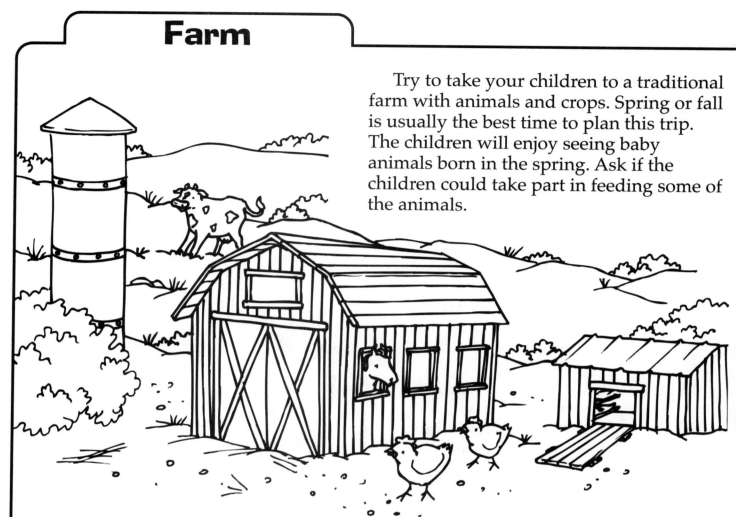

Tips

- 🏠 Teach the children some simple safety rules to use when they are around farm animals.

- 🏠 Ask if someone would demonstrate how certain farm equipment works.

- 🏠 Try to arrange a wagon ride around the farm.

- 🏠 Take bags for dirty shoes or put bags over the children's shoes and secure with rubber bands to make disposable rubber boots.

Related Books

Barn Dance, Bill Martin and John Archambault, (Henry Holt, 1991).

Big Red Barn, Margaret Wise Brown, (HarperCollins Children's, 1995).

The Day Jimmy's Boa Ate the Wash, Trinka Hakes Noble, (Puffin Books, 1984).

"Not Now!" Said the Cow, Joanne F. Oppenheim, (Bantam Books, 1989).

Old MacDonald's Farm, Kate Taylor, (McClanahan, 1994).

Counting Book

Make farm animal counting books. Draw a simple barn shape pattern. Use it to make an 11-page book for each child. On the cover of each book print, "My Farm Animal Counting Book."

Print a number 1 on the first page, a 2 on the second page, and so on up to 10 on the last page. Set out colored ink pads and rubber stamps of various farm animals— cow, horse, sheep, pig, goat, turkey, duck, goose, rooster, and chicken.

Let each child choose one farm animal to stamp on the first page, two animals to stamp on the second page, and so on.

Let each child share his or her book. Have the rest of the children count aloud 1 through 10 as the child turns the pages.

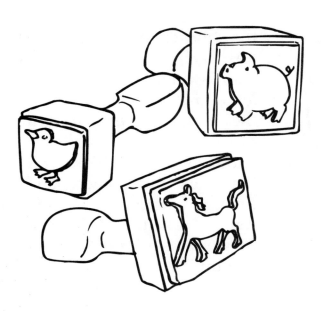

Corncob Art

Cook corn on the cob for a snack. Boil the corn with a small amount of sugar for a tasty treat! Wash and save the cobs. Let them air dry.

Give each child a large cow shape made from white drawing paper. Let the children paint the cows brown by rolling dry corncobs in a small amount of tempera paint, and then rolling the paint on the paper. After the paint dries, let the children use black markers to make spots, eyes, noses, and mouths on their cows.

Farm

Barnyard Movement

Talk with your children about the different ways farm animals move and the sounds they make. Then have the children line up outside. Tell them to pretend that you are the farmer and they are farm animals. You want them to go from "the pasture" to "the barnyard" (choose a designated place). Call out the name of a farm animal. When you do, have the children go to the designated place, moving and sounding like that animal. Take the children back to the pasture by repeating the same activity and calling out the name of a different animal.

Barnyard Dance

Play a recording of "Old MacDonald Had a Farm." Have the children join hands and form a circle. As they sing the chorus, have them circle to the left and then to the right. As they sing each verse, have them move to the center of the circle and back holding hands. Have them raise their joined hands up high when they reach the center. Make up other dance movements after the children accomplish these simple steps.

Farm Animal Sorting

Cut out pictures of a cow, a horse, a sheep, a pig, a chicken, a rooster, a duck, a goose, a turkey, a dog, a cat, a mouse, and any other farm animals you can find.

Form two large circles with yarn. Choose two categories, one for each circle (for example, big and little, two legs and four legs, fur and feathers, etc.). Have the children help you place the pictures in the appropriate circles. Change the categories and sort the animals again.

The Farmer in the Dell Role-Play Fun

Make a simple headband to represent each character (farmer, wife, child, nurse, dog, cat, rat, cheese) in the song "The Farmer in the Dell."

Choose children to wear the headbands. Have the children join hands and form a circle. Ask the farmer to stand in the center of the circle. Have the children march around the farmer as they sing. When the children sing the second verse, have the wife join the farmer in the center while the children march and sing. Continue this activity with each character. When singing the last verse, have the cheese stand alone in the center and have the rest of the characters rejoin the circle.

Cheese Cube Snacks

Cut small cubes of different cheeses and place them on a platter. Set out crackers. Give each child a paper plate. Let the children nibble on crackers and cheese.

Feed Store

This trip is especially fun for children who live in the city. They can see different kinds of huge equipment and special tools used by farmers and ranchers.

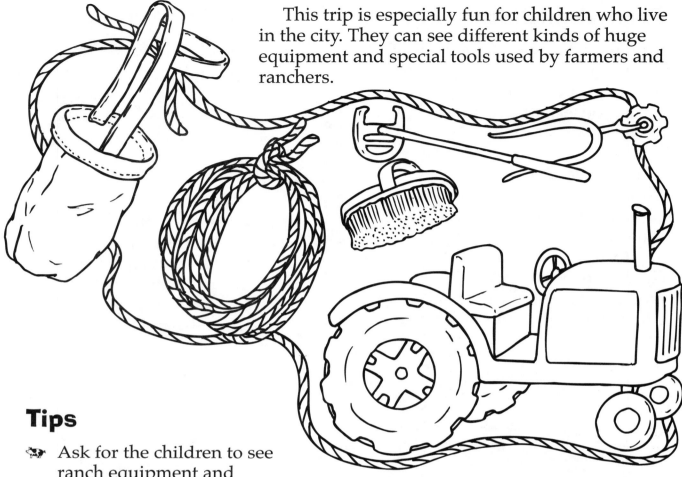

Tips

🐄 Ask for the children to see ranch equipment and supplies. Ranch companies will have large tractors and earth-moving equipment.

🐄 Ask for a demonstration of various kinds of equipment.

🐄 Compare the sizes of tires. See how many children will fit in the hub of a large tire.

🐄 If possible, find a feed store that has feed sacks with the pictures of the animals on the outside of the bags so the children that do not read will become aware of all the different kinds of feed.

🐄 Ask someone to explain the use of tack, medical materials, calf bottles, ropes, brands, chaps, spurs, and other types of ranch supplies.

🐄 Ask for a roping demonstration if the store has rodeo practice equipment.

🐄 Ask for free calendars, rain gauges, fly swatters, or other inexpensive items for the children to take home to help remember their trip.

Sand Table Fun

Place toy tractors in the sandbox area. Fill the water table with dirt and place toy trucks and tractors on the table. Let the children have fun pretending to be ranch hands working with big equipment.

Tractor Tracks

Cover the tables with newspaper. Give each child a sheet of paper. Set out shallow containers of different colors of tempera paint. Let the children roll toy tractors through the paints and then on the paper to make tractor track designs.

Related Books

Baby Farm Animals, Garth Williams, (Golden Book, 1998).

The Farm, Tessa Krailing, (Barron's Educational Series, 1991).

Meanwhile Back at the Ranch, Trinka Hakes Noble, (Puffin, 1992).

Picking Apples and Pumpkins, Amy and Richard Hutchings, (Scholastic, 1994).

Feed Store

Seed Pictures

Feed stores will usually sell you
small amounts of garden seeds.
Give each child a piece of sturdy
paper. Let the children arrange and
glue the seeds on the paper to
make seed collages.

Trail Mix Snack

Let your children help you stir up a
granola or trail mix that combines
oats or oat cereal, wheat and corn
cereals, sunflower seeds, corn nuts,
peanuts, and other foods that are
eaten by both people and animals.
Let the children nibble this treat
while you read a farm story.

The Tractor on the Farm

Sung to: "Wheels on the Bus"

The tractor on the farm
Goes back and forth,
Back and forth,
Back and forth.
The tractor on the farm
Goes back and forth,
Early in the morning!

Marsha Elyn Wright

Roping Fun

Tape together the ends of a short length of clothesline to form a large ring or circle. Make several of these rings. Set up chairs outside to represent cattle. Let each child practice "roping cattle" by trying to toss a ring onto the back of a chair. When a child succeeds, he or she gets to yell, "Yahoo!"

Tire Snacks

Set out tire-shaped crackers and cheese and carrot rounds on a large pizza pan. Let the children turn the "tire" as they help themselves to these healthy snacks.

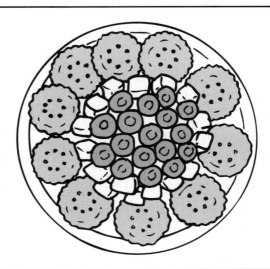

Fire Department

This trip provides a wonderful opportunity for young children to learn about fire safety and to see what a firefighter does each day. Fire stations usually welcome school groups and have well-prepared presentations. Firefighters can usually bring a small truck to school and do a small demonstration at school.

Tips

 Before your trip, tell the children that if an alarm sounds, they will have to move quickly to a safe area. The firefighters will have to leave in a hurry.

 Ask the firefighter to demonstrate equipment and firefighter gear.

 Tell the children that the living area is just like a firefighter's home away from home. Remind the children to keep their hands to their sides.

 If the station has an EMT unit, ask to see the inside of the unit.

Related Books

I Am a Firefighter, Cynthia Benjamin, (Barron's Educational Series, 1995).

Fire, Fire, Said Mrs. McGuire, Bill Martin, (Harcourt Brace, 1996).

The Fire Station, Robert N. Munsch, (Firefly Books, 1991).

Fire Engines, Anne F. Rockwell, (Dutton Children's Books, 1986).

Who's at the Fire House?, Bettina Peterson, (Putman Publishing, 1996).

Stop, Drop, and Roll

Practice "Stop, Drop, and Roll" and "Stay Low and Go" before you go and when you return. Let the children practice these movements in a large area first and then in the classroom.

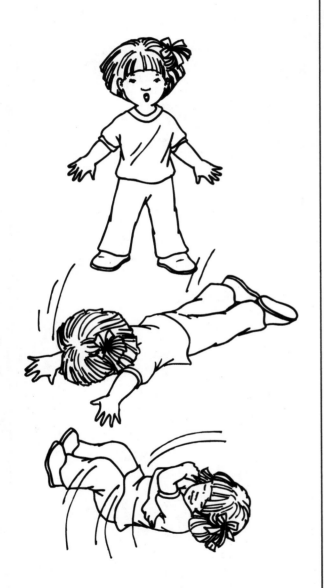

Fire Drill Practice

Have a practice fire drill at school. Establish specific procedures and rules with your children so they know how to behave and where the assigned place of safety is. Send information home about fire safety and encourage fire drills in the home.

Fire Department

Fire Scene Mural

Tape a long sheet of blue butcher paper on a wall. Tape brown paper buildings on the background. Let the children paint flames using red and yellow paint. Cut out firefighting equipment and vehicles from magazines and tape them on the background. Talk about the mural when the children are finished.

Role-Playing

Set up an area with a cardboard box house, water hoses, plastic firefighter hats, yellow raincoats, and rubber boots so the children can pretend to be firefighters. Put out toy fire trucks and ambulances if you have them.

Stop Then Drop Then Roll Away

Sung to: "Twinkle, Twinkle, Little Star"

If you know the safety rule,
Fires will not frighten you.
Stop, then drop, then roll away,
Above your head the smoke
   will stay,
After dialing 911,
Firefighters quickly come!

Marsha Elyn Wright

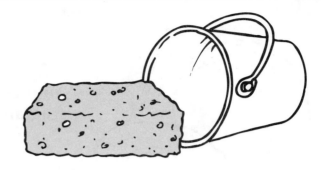

Put-Out-the-Fire Relay

Place your children into small relay teams. Give each team a large sponge and a pail of water. A short distance from each team, place an empty pail. Tell the children that at your signal, the first person on each team is to place his or her sponge in the water, trying to absorb lots of water. That person will then run with the water-soaked sponge to the team's empty pail and squeeze the water into it. That child will run back to the next person in line on his or her team to repeat the activity.

After all the children have had a turn, measure how much water each team was able to squeeze into the empty pails!

Red Snacks

Provide a "red" snack (gelatin, frosted cookies, cheese, strawberry jam on crackers, strawberry flavored milk) for the children to eat.

Florist

This trip is a wonderful experience, especially around Valentine's Day. Most shops will have a large variety of balloons, flowers, and small gifts. Your children will enjoy the variety of colorful, fragrant flowers.

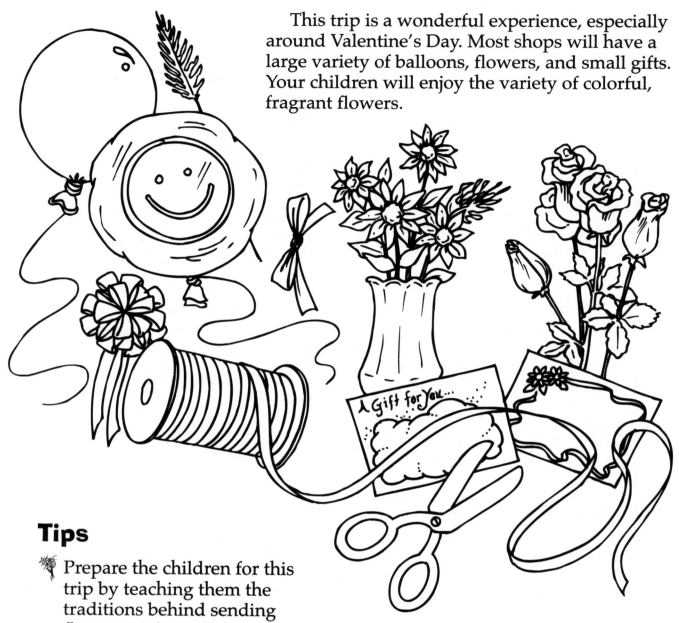

A Gift for You...

Tips

🌸 Prepare the children for this trip by teaching them the traditions behind sending flowers and sweet gifts.

🌸 Ask the florist to demonstrate floral arranging and bow making.

🌸 Visit the cool room where the cut flowers are stored.

🌸 Ask the florist to save some unwanted flowers for the children to touch and smell.

🌸 Stress to your children that they need to keep their hands to their sides.

🌸 Remind your children that they may touch or smell flowers only when instructed to do so.

🌸 Check for plant allergies before planning this trip.

Flower Shop Fun

Set up a pretend floral shop with silk flowers, plastic containers, and lots of ribbons. Don't forget the play cash register, play money, and note paper for taking orders and receipts.

I'm a Little Flower

Sung to: "I'm a Little Teapot"

I'm a little flower,
Soft and blue,
Here are my green leaves,
The sun shines through.
When the day is over,
Then I fall.
Morning comes, I stand up tall!

Marsha Elyn Wright

Flower Cards

Give each child a folded sheet of colored paper to use to make a card for his or her parents. Let the children arrange and glue cutout pictures of flowers from seed catalogs, used greeting cards, and calendars.

Just for You!

Related Books

Alison's Zinna, Anita Lobel, (William Morrow, 1996).

Flowers for Mommy, Susan Anderson, (Africa World Press, 1995).

The Reason for a Flower, Ruth Heller, (Paper Star Books, 1999).

The Rose in My Garden, Arnold Lobel, (William Morrow, 1993).

Florist

Peach Flower Snack

Place peach slices in a flower shape around a dab of cottage cheese. Cherries or pineapple can be placed on top of the cottage cheese. Make one peach flower for each child.

Floral Sorting

Cut out various colors and sizes of magazine pictures of flowers. Make a sorting and classifying activity using the colors of the flowers. Form circles with lengths of yarn. Let the children place pictures showing flowers of similar colors inside the same circle.

Guess How Many Leaves

Put several leaves inside a glass jar. Have the children try to guess how many leaves are in the jar. Record their guesses. Then count the leaves as you remove them from the jar. Check to see which guesses were too high or too low. Let the children help you count the leaves as you put them back into the jar.

Funny Leaf Stories

Collect a variety of leaves. Give each child a sheet of construction paper, glue, and felt tip markers. Let each child choose a leaf to glue onto his or her paper. Have the children use markers to add funny face and body features to their leaves. Then ask each child to tell you a little story about his or her leaf. Record this story on a small strip of paper. Glue the story below the leaf.

Ask the children if you can share their stories with the class.

Flower Match

Collect five pairs of different kinds of flowers. Press the flowers between the pages of heavy books for several days. This will squeeze out the excess moisture. Mount each flower on a square of sturdy paper and cover the paper with clear, self-stick paper.

Mix up the papers and place them on a table. Let the children take turns matching the pairs of flowers.

Grocery Store

All the children have probably been shopping for food with their parents, but few, if any, will have seen the areas not open to the public. These are the areas you will want them to see and experience.

Tips

- Call ahead and set up an appointment during the least busy time of the day. Ask to speak to the person who will lead the tour so you can talk with him or her about what you want your children to experience.

- Ask to see the truck loading ramp, the freezer room, the meat storage cooler, the produce area, the warehouse staging area, and the bakery.

- Ask for a demonstration on how meat is trimmed and wrapped.

- Ask if the store has a one-way mirror that overlooks the entire store. Ask if the children can view the store from that mirror.

- Ask if food will be served to the children. If food will be served, make sure you check for food allergies. If a child is allergic to peanut butter, make sure the bakery is not baking peanut butter cookies that day.

Grocery Store Fun

Set up a grocery store in your classroom. Gather empty food boxes and containers and some real fruits and vegetables. Include a play cash register, play money, and, if possible, toy grocery carts. Let the children take turns role-playing shoppers, clerks, and cashiers.

Related Books

Barney and Baby Bop Go to the Grocery Store, Donna D. Cooner, (Lyrick Publishing, 1997).

My Little Supermarket, Caroline Repchuk, (Millbrook Press, 1997).

One Day at the Supermarket, Donna Bryant, (Ideal Publications, 1989).

Tommy at the Grocery Store, Bill Grossman, (HarperCollins, 1991).

Sorting Groceries Game

Make a sorting game of pictures of things people could buy in a supermarket. Place on a table a paper bag and several pictures of things found in a grocery store and items not found there. Have one child at a time pick up a picture, say the name of the item, and tell if it can be found in a grocery store. If it is a grocery item, have the child place the picture in the paper bag.

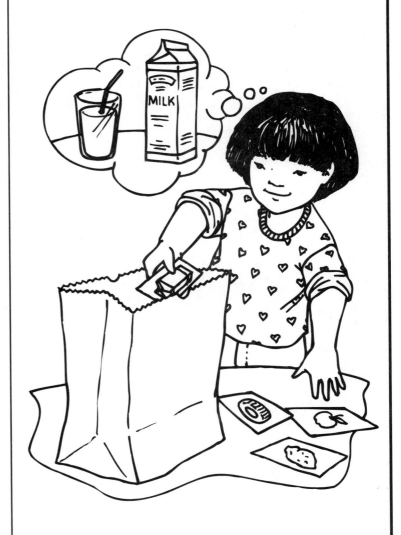

Grocery Store

A Tasting Party

Purchase some unusual vegetables and fruits and have a tasting party. Display them and talk about the different tastes of sweet, sour, bitter, and salty. Let the children sample the ones they want. Vote on the favorites!

Fruit and Veggie Plates

Give each child a paper plate. Display small pictures of fruits and vegetables cut out of magazines. Let the children help you identify the names of the fruits and vegetables. Have the children glue different fruits and vegetables on their paper plates. Encourage the children to share with their families the names of the fruits and vegetables glued on their plates.

Fruit Prints

Slice a variety of fruits (apples, oranges, etc.) in half. Pour different colors of paint onto several sponges set in pie tins. The paint will be absorbed, and the sponges will act as ink pads.

Let the children press different fruit halves on the sponges and gently press them on construction paper to make fruits prints.

Grocery Carts Are Rolling

Sung to: "Eensy, Weensy Spider"

Our grocery cart is rolling fast,
Up and down the aisles,
Put in some carrots,
And some apple pies,
Stop at the check out,
Tally up the bill,
Then we take the food to our
     house,
And eat and have our fill!

Marsha Elyn Wright

Applesauce Snack

Peel and cut up three to four sweet apples. Place the apple pieces in a sauce pan. Add ½ cup water. Sprinkle cinnamon and nutmeg to taste. Cover and simmer about 20 minutes, until the apples are tender. Let the children mash the cooked apples with a potato masher. Cool the applesauce. Place dollops of applesauce inside small paper cups, add spoons, and eat!

Hospital

A tour of a hospital or a doctor's office can be exciting for young children and help calm their fears about doctors and nurses. Choose the location that will have the best tour for your age children.

Tips

🚑 If you choose to visit a hospital, ask if they routinely give these tours and what the tours include.

🚑 Ask if a special tour for young children can be changed if you do not feel the regular tour meets your children's needs.

🚑 If you choose to visit a doctor's office, talk with the staff ahead of time to learn what they will be showing the children.

🚑 Ask a doctor or nurse to put on a gown, a mask, and gloves in front of the children so they can see a medical uniform.

🚑 Tell the children that no one will be treated at the doctor's office or hospital. This is just a visit.

🚑 At either location, stress to the children not to touch any equipment and to listen closely and politely.

🚑 Ask to see an X-ray displayed on a lighted box.

Related Books

About the Hospital

Curious George Goes to the Hospital, Margret and H.A. Rey, (Houghton Mifflin, 1976).

Going to the Hospital, Anne Civardi, (E D C P, 1993).

The Hospital Scares Me, Paula Z. Hogan, (Raintree, 1992).

Max's Daddy Goes to the Hospital, Danielle Steele, (Delacorte Press, 1989).

About the Doctor's Office

The Berenstain Bears Go to the Doctor, Stan Berenstain, (Demco Media, 1981).

My Doctor, My Friend, Patrick K. Hallinan, (Hambleton, 1996).

My First Doctor Visit, Julia Allen, (A R O Publishing Co., 1988).

Hello, Doctor

Sung to: "Frère Jacques"

Hello, Doctor,
Hello, Doctor,
I am sick,
I am sick.
Help my body get well,
Help my body get well,
Won't you, please?
Won't you, please?

Little sick one,
Little sick one,
Don't be sad,
Don't be sad.
Medicine and sleeping,
Medicine and sleeping,
Will help you,
Will help you.

Marsha Elyn Wright

Hospital

Counting Game

Make a counting game using tongue depressors. Collect small plastic food trays. On each tray, print a number. Set out tongue depressors. Let the children take turns placing the correct amount of tongue depressors in the trays.

Healthy Activities Mural

Talk with your children about activities that will help keep their bodies healthy—eat healthy foods, exercise daily, get plenty of rest, wash regularly, laugh, and play. Cut out magazine pictures of these activities. Mount a large sheet of colored paper on a wall. Let the children choose pictures to glue on the paper. Then have the children draw pictures of themselves doing the activities with their families. This is a favorite display for parents!

Stick Sculptures

Let the children use tongue depressors and tape to make sculptures. Mount each sculpture on a sturdy sheet of paper. Let each child name his or her sculpture.

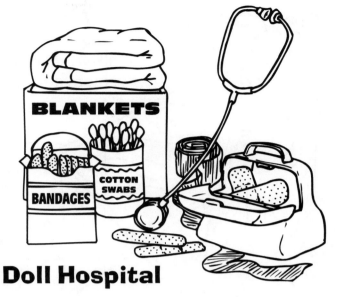

Doll Hospital

Set up a hospital for dolls. Place toy medical bags and equipment in an area. Set out adhesive bandages, cloth bandages, doll blankets, and other pint-size medical supplies. Let the children take turns helping the dolls "get well."

Healthy Shakes

Tell the children that in order to help keep their bodies healthy, it's important to eat healthy foods. Make a healthy fruit shake for each child to sample. Mix 4 cups of milk, 4 sliced bananas, and 4 scoops of frozen yogurt together in a blender. Pour this frothy shake into small paper cups for your children to enjoy!

Kite Store

The best kite stores are usually found in beach front or lake front communities. Young children are very excited about visiting kite stores and seeing all the different colors and shapes of the kites.

Tips

- If possible, arrange for a demonstration of the flying of a large kite.

- If a demonstration is not possible, check out a video of stunt kite flying.

- Before you take this field trip, construct a simple kite from a kit with the children. Discuss the purpose of each part.

- Plan this trip in the spring or early summer for the best possible weather in which to observe a kite-flying demonstration.

Related Books

Curious George Flies a Kite, H.A. and Margret Rey, (Houghton Mifflin, 1977).

The Dragon Kite, Nancy Luenn, (Harcourt Brace, 1993).

Go Fly a Kite, Ray Brock, (Bookstore, 1976).

Kite in the Park, Lucy Cousins, (Candlewick Press, 1992).

Merle the High Flying Squirrel, Bill Peet, (Houghton Mifflin, 1983).

Blotto Kites

Give each child a kite-shaped piece of construction paper folded in half lengthwise. Have the children unfold the kites and use eyedroppers to squeeze drops of paint on one side of the kites. Have the children refold the kites and rub their hands gently across the paper.

Tell the children to open up their kites to see the interesting designs made by the drops of paint. Tape lengths of yarn to the kites for kite tails. Let the children tape paper bows on their kite tails. Attach kite strings and let the children take their kites outside to watch them flutter in the wind.

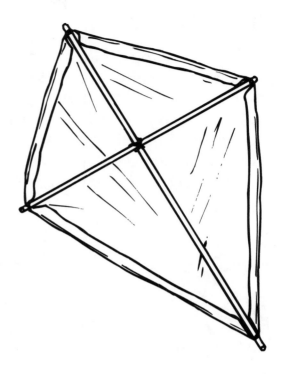

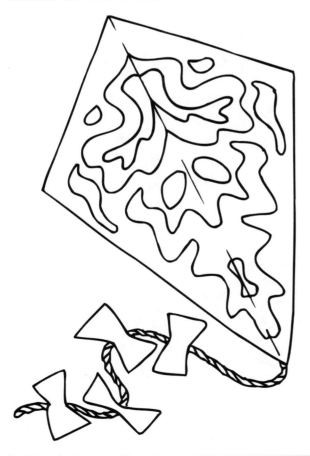

Trash Bag Kites

Make simple kites from plastic trash bags and small dowel rods. Cut small kite shapes out of the plastic trash bags. Tape one thin dowel lengthwise and one dowel crosswise on each kite. Tie long lengths of string around the dowels where they intersect on each kite.

Let the children securely tape lengths of fabric strips on their kites to make kite tails. Let the children take their kites outside on a windy day. Help them try to fly their kites and to observe a kite flying in the wind. Ask questions such as "What happens when the wind stops blowing?" and "What happens when you pull in your string?"

Kite Store

Kite Match-Ups

Make a matching game from scraps of fabric or wallpaper. Cut the scraps into about 10 kite shapes. Mount each kite on cardboard and cut each in half lengthwise. Mix up the halves and let the children match up the kite halves.

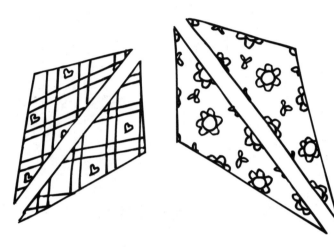

Kite-Shaped Snacks

Cut toast that has been buttered and jellied into triangles. Each child can put two triangles together to make a kite shape. The children can eat these for a yummy morning snack!

Move Like Kites

Place the children in pairs. Give each pair of children one long length of thick yarn or ribbon. Have one child in each pair pretend to be a kite and the other child pretend to be a kite flyer.

In each pair, have the "kite" hold onto one end of the yarn and the "kite flyer" hold the other end. Let the "kite flyers" reel their kites in and out while the "kites" move and dart about in the wind. Then have the children trade places with their partners.

Kites Are Flying

Sung to: "Frère Jacques"

Kites are flying,
Kites are flying,
Way up high,
Way up high,
Spinning round in circles,
Spinning round in circles,
In the sky,
In the sky!

Marsha Elyn Wright

Kite Tail Counting

Cut 10 kite shapes out of construction paper. Attach a yarn kite tail to each kite. Mount the kites on a bulletin board. Randomly print the number 1 on one kite, 2 on another kite, and so on up to the number 10.

Cut 55 bows out of paper. Let the children take turns attaching the correct number of bows to the kite tails.

Lumberyard

Young children will enjoy visiting such an active place! They will like watching workers saw, stack, and move lumber and other building materials.

Tips

- Check with the lumberyard to see if they are set up to have young children visit.

- Ask for a demonstration of sawing and stacking lumber.

- Have the children wear shoes, not sandals. Particles and other scraps of building materials might injure toes in sandals.

- Remind the children to keep their hands to themselves.

- Ask for small samples of any building materials or scraps of wood. Be sure to talk about safe handling of cut wood to avoid splinters.

- Bring a pail or sturdy bag to collect wood curls and sawdust.

- Ask for a demonstration on measuring doors, window frames, and other building materials.

Wood Shaving Masks

Set out a box of wood shavings or curls. Give each child a large paper plate. Cut two holes for eyes in each plate. Have each child draw and color a face on the plate. Let the children glue wood curls on their plates for hair, eyebrows, mustaches, and other features. Glue a large tongue depressor to each mask.

Carpentry Corner

Set up an area where the children can play with wood. Collect plastic toy hammers, screwdrivers, nails, and other tools as well as wood blocks and tape measures.

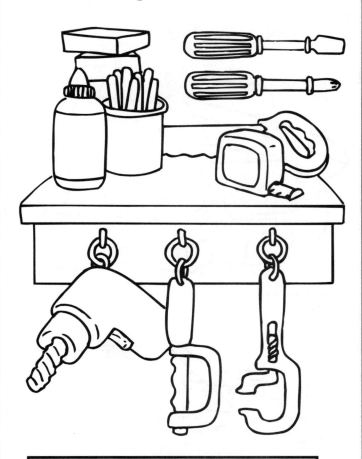

Related Books

Forest Log, James R. Newton, (Harper and Row, 1980).

From Tree to Table, Ali Mitgutsch, (Carolrhoda, 1981).

Little Fir Tree, Margaret Wise Brown, (Harper, 1985).

Story of Paul Bunyan, Barbara Emberley, (Prentice-Hall, 1963).

Lumberyard

Build and Paint

Let the children use wood blocks and toy tools to construct a "building" outside the classroom. Give the children large paintbrushes and pails of water and let them "paint" their finished building.

Sawdust Paperweight

Mix together 2½ cups sawdust, ½ cup wheat paste, and about 12 cups of water. Cut plastic foam balls in half so that each child gets one half. Let the children shape the mixture around the plastic foam halves. Let dry for several days.

Have the children use tempera paints to make designs on their paperweights. Let the children give their decorative gifts to their moms and dads.

Wood Sorting Game

Cut out magazine pictures of items made from wood and items not made from wood. Have the children take turns sorting the pictures into two groups.

Build a House

Sung to: "The Mulberry Bush"

This is the way
We build a house,
Build a house, build a house.
This is the way
We build a house,
With hammer, wood, and nails.

This is the way
We paint a house,
Paint a house, paint a house.
This is the way
We paint a house,
With ladder, paint, and brush.

Marsha Elyn Wright

Treats From Trees

Slice and cut up different foods that grow on trees. Include foods such as apples, oranges, bananas, and nuts. Surprise the children by setting out chocolate, which comes from the seeds of the cacao tree! Let the children sample these tree treats!

Music Shop

All children love to make music. So young children will really enjoy this trip. It's especially fun for vision-impaired and disabled children. Most music stores sell band instruments, and some stores stock very unusual drums and rhythm instruments.

Tips

♫ This is a good trip to plan in the winter months when cold or stormy weather makes it difficult to be outdoors.

♫ Visit the store and see what kinds of instruments it sells.

♫ Ask if someone will demonstrate how various instruments are played.

♫ Find out the best days and times to visit the store so you are not there when it is busy with customers.

♫ Let the children look through school supply catalogs to see all the different kinds of musical instruments. Cut out the pictures and make a collage for your classroom.

♫ Survey the parents to see if anyone would play an instrument for the children at school. This will increase the interest of the children before and after you take the trip.

This Is the Way

Have the children parade around the room as they sing and act out this song.

Sung to: "The Mulberry Bush"

This is the way
We tap the drum,
Tap the drum,
Tap the drum.
This is the way
We tap the drum,
In our musical marching band.

This is the way
We blow the horn,
Blow the horn,
Blow the horn.
This is the way
We blow the horn,
In our musical marching band.

Marsha Elyn Wright

Copy Cat Rhythms

Give each child a drum, a pair of rhythm sticks, a triangle, or other simple musical instrument to tap or beat. Tell the children that they are to copy the rhythm you tap out. Start with simple rhythms. Ask for volunteers to tap out a rhythm that the rest of the children can copy.

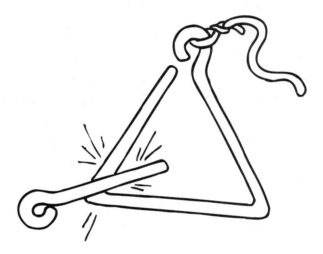

Related Books

The Happy Hedgehog Band, Martin Waddell, (Candlewick Press, 1994).

Kids Make Music!: Clapping and Tapping from Bach to Rock!, Avery Hart, Paul Mantell, Loretta Trezzo Braren, (Williamson Publishing, 1993).

Max Found Two Sticks, Brian Pinkney, (Simon & Schuster, 1997).

Snake Alley Band, Elizabeth Nygaard, (Bantam Doubleday Dell Books for Young Readers, 1998).

Zin!Zin!Zin!: A Violin, Lloyd Moss, (Simon & Schuster, 1995).

Music Shop

Music Makers

Ask for parent volunteers to bring in any musical instruments that they can talk about with the children. If this isn't possible, cut out pictures of musical instruments and display them. Discuss with the children how the sounds are created (examples—blowing air on a reed, plucking a string, hitting a surface, strumming strings, etc.).

Musical Match

Make a memory game using stickers of musical instruments. Collect 10 pairs of matching stickers of musical instruments. Attach each sticker to half of an index card. Mix up the cards. Let the children find the matching musical instruments.

Rhythm Shakers

Give each child a toilet tissue tube. Have the children paint or color designs on the tubes. Close up one end of each tube by attaching masking tape strips over the opening. Put one or two spoonfuls of rice in each tube and attach tape to the open end to close it up securely. Play marching music and let the children parade around the room, shaking their rhythm instruments!

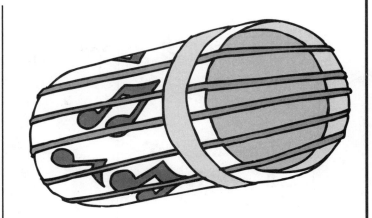

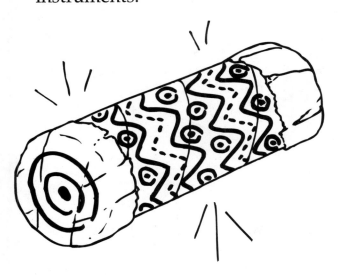

Marching Band

Collect empty oatmeal containers, cardboard tubes, rubber bands, small plastic combs, and tissue. Help the children stretch rubber bands over the openings of the containers. Help them wrap tissue around the combs. Let the children pluck the rubber bands and hum through the tissue-wrapped combs to make musical sounds while they march around the room.

Drum Snacks

Set up a snack of large "drum" snacks. Spread large crackers with peanut butter. On each cracker, lay a set of carrot sticks to form the "drumsticks" for each drum.

Neighborhood

This is another trip with endless possibilities! Your children will enjoy discovering the changes in nature happening in their neighborhood. This trip will alert them to things happening around your school.

Tips

🏫 Drive or walk the area weekly or monthly. Look for signs of the seasons, buildings under construction or destruction, landscaping projects, gardens, and new stores opening.

🏫 Take a walk at the start of a new season. Identify specific trees, gardens, and buildings to observe during each trip. Tell the children to note the changes taking place with these trees, flowers, and other specific things in the neighborhood. Record these changes by taking pictures.

🏫 If there is a construction project, walk by frequently and note changes. Ask for scraps of wood for projects at school. Take a camera and take pictures of different steps of the construction.

🏫 Take a litter walk. Have the children wear plastic gloves and pick up litter around the schoolyard.

🏫 Teach a lesson about traffic safety before you leave the schoolyard.

The Changing Seasons

Make a poster showing the changes in nature during each season. Draw two lines to divide the poster into four sections. Label each section with the name of a season—Fall, Winter, Spring, and Summer. Let the children mount photographs taken on each field trip in the appropriate section. (Your children can also post seasonal pictures cut from magazines.) By the end of the school year, the poster should have four sets of pictures.

Building Going Up!

If there is a construction site, make a poster that shows the progress noted on each walk. Take photographs of the progress and let the children mount the photos on the poster. Ask the children to help you label each photograph.

Related Books

About the Neighborhood, (Brighter Vision, 1998).

I Got Community, Melrose Cooper, (Henry Holt, 1995).

In My Neighborhood, Karen Backstein, (Scholastic, 1993).

Neighborhood ODEs, Gary Soto, (Scholastic, 1994).

See You Around, Sam!, Lois Lowery, (Houghton Mifflin, 1996).

Neighborhood

Litter Monster Bags

Decorate large paper bags to look like "Litter Monsters." Let each child make a Litter Monster bag. Line each bag with a plastic grocery sack. Let the children take the bags home to keep in family cars or in back yards.

Take a class Litter Monster bag on a litter walk. Challenge your children to fill it. Remember that the children who pick up trash should be wearing gloves. (You can also have adults pick up the litter the children find.)

Build a Neighborhood

Cover a small table with a plastic tablecloth. Make streets with wide masking tape. Let the children make a model of a neighborhood using small blocks, toy vehicles, and tiny plastic trees and bushes.

Walking Tubes

Collect one long empty, cardboard, wrapping paper tube for each child. (Ask parents to help you.)

Give each child a tube. Let the children paint designs on their tubes to personalize them. Let them dry. Print each child's name on his or her tube. Let the children use their "walking tubes" as they hike together on a short trip around the neighborhood.

Sing a Song of Seasons

Sung to: "Sing a Song of Sixpence"

Sing a song of seasons,
Let's name the four we know,
Winter, spring, and *summer,*
Fall is how they go.

When the year is over,
Oh, they begin again,
Winter, spring, and summer, fall—
It's time to start again!

Marsha Elyn Wright

Build-a-House Snacks

Give each child a slice of bread to make a house. Let the children spread peanut butter on the bread to "paint" their houses. Have the children use carrot sticks and squares of cheese to make "doors," "windows," and "chimneys."

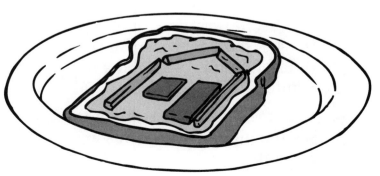

Newspaper Office

Small publications can be just as rewarding and interesting as huge production newspaper businesses. Call around and see what possibilities are available in your area. As an option, check to see if your local school district has a print shop that publishes newsletters and handbooks. This also makes a fun, educational field trip for young children.

Tips

- Check out the location for safety and space so your young children can move about easily.

- Ask for scraps of paper that can be used for art projects.

- Prepare the children for the noise and smells. Stress safety.

- If possible, arrange for a step-by-step tour of how an article or invitation is prepared and printed.

- Visit the photo department to see the high-tech cameras, if possible.

Related Books

The Furry News: How to Make a Newspaper, Loreen Leddy, (Holiday House, 1996).

Paperboy, Mary Kay Kroeger and Lisa Borden, (Houghton Mifflin, 1996).

Newspaper Capers, Michael Lenhart, (Learning Works, 1994).

The Newspaper Kids, Juanita Phillips, (HarperCollins, 1998).

The Tram to Bondi Beach, Elizabeth Hathorn and Julie Vivas, (Kane-Mille, 1989).

Newspaper Corner

Set up a newspaper corner. Put a typewriter, office stamps, play camera, alphabet stamps, paper, a child's printing kit, and other office supplies in the center. Let the children have fun pretending to be reporters.

Scissor Practice

Put newspaper classified ads and scissors in a center. Let the children practice using scissors by having them cut out the ads along the solid line boxes. Mount a sheet of large poster paper and title it "Want Ads." Let the children glue their cut-out ads on the poster.

Newspaper Office

Letter Match-Up

Cut out pairs of alphabet letters from newspaper headlines that use large print. Mount each letter on an index card. Mix up the cards. Let the children take turns matching the letters.

Class Newspaper

Let the children create a class newspaper. Make a sentence frame similar to the following: "Here is news from our home. _____ has a new _____. (or) _____ is going to _____." Copy this sentence frame on half-sheets of paper and give each child one form. Tell the children to take the forms home. Send home a note that asks the parents to help the children complete the form. Gather and compile all the "articles" into a class newspaper.

Funny Newspaper Hats

Make funny hats from newspaper. Help each child roll a folded sheet of newspaper into a cone and secure with tape. Let the children decorate their hats with markers, crayons, and construction paper strips.

We Are Reading

Sung to: "Frère Jacques"

We are reading,
We are reading,
Newspapers,
Newspapers,
Classifieds
And comics,
Sports and feature stories,
News, news, news,
News, news, news.

Marsha Elyn Wright

Newspaper Placemats

Let each child decorate a folded sheet of newspaper to make a place mat. Set out construction paper strips and scraps, glue, scissors, crayons, and other decorative supplies. Cover each placemat with clear self-stick paper. Then set out a snack of crackers and cheese to eat on the festive placemats.

Optometrist

This trip is so important because it will be the first exposure to an eye doctor for many children. It can be a fun yet educational trip that will calm the fears of many children. If possible, choose a doctor who has young children or who likes working with young children.

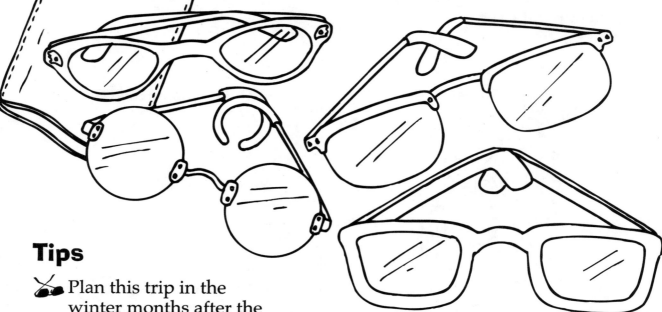

Tips

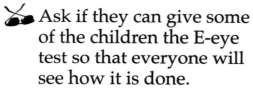

- Plan this trip in the winter months after the back-to-school rush to the doctor's office.

- Ask if they can give some of the children the E-eye test so that everyone will see how it is done.

- Ask the person leading your group to stress eye safety.

- Ask if there is anything written in Braille for the children to see and touch.

- Ask for folding paper sunglasses for each child.

Related Books

Arthur's Eyes, Marc Brown, (Little, Brown, 1986).

Chimps Don't Wear Glasses, Laura J. Numeroff, (Simon & Schuster, 1998).

Glasses, Bob Reese, (Children's Press, 1992).

Glasses—Who Needs 'Em?, Lane Smith, (Vikings, 1991).

Mr. Fine Goes to the Eye Doctor, Michael L. Sirken, (Sirken Publishing, 1993).

Spectacles, Ellen Raskin, (Simon & Schuster, 1972).

Grandma's and Grandpa's Glasses Finger Play

Teach the children this favorite finger play. Have the children use thumbs and pointer fingers to form the glasses, touch their fingertips together over their heads to form the hat, and place their hands in their laps at the end of the first verse. They can fold their arms across their chests at the end of the second verse.

Here are Grandma's glasses,
Here is Grandma's hat,
Here's the way,
She folds her hands,
And puts them in her lap.

Here are Grandpa's glasses,
Here is Grandpa's hat,
Here's the way,
He folds his arms,
Just like that!

Traditional

Blindfold Game

Ask your children for volunteers to be blindfolded and use their senses of touch, smell, and hearing to try to identify their friends and familiar objects. After playing the game, talk about the importance of taking care of your eyes.

Optometrist

Cellophane Glasses

Let the children make some big funny glasses from posterboard and colored cellophane paper. Cut an eyewear frame out of thin posterboard for each child. Cut scraps of colored cellophane. Let the children choose colors of cellophane to tape across the openings of their "glasses."

Matching Game

Make an eyeglass matching game. First, cut out magazine pictures of eye frames that have simple geometric shapes. Or, draw eyeglass frames using simple geometric shapes. Then cut out simple geometric shapes—circles, squares, rectangles, ovals, and diamonds—from construction paper. Let the children take turns matching the shapes of the frames to the construction paper shapes.

A Special Visitor

Try to arrange to have a blind person visit your class. If possible, have him or her bring a seeing-eye dog. Ask your visitor to demonstrate the importance of a seeing-eye dog. Ask if he or she will show the children the special watches, clocks, and other items that make everyday living easier for a blind person.

Wearing Some Glasses

Sung to: "Mary Wore Her Red Dress"

_____ wearing some glasses,
Glasses, glasses,
_____ wearing some glasses,
All day long.

Marsha Elyn Wright

Use a different child's name each time you sing a verse. Let the child you sing about wear a pair of toy eyeglasses.

Sweet Treat

Use thin red licorice sticks to make an eyeglass frame for each child. Place the licorice eyeglasses on paper plates for a sweet treat!

Park

This trip provides a wonderful opportunity for young children to explore nature in a safe environment.

NATURE TRAIL

Tips

🍁 Before your trip, check to see if the park has safe playground equipment for young children as well as a picnic area.

🍁 Check to see if the park has clean, accessible bathrooms.

🍁 Have each child wear safe, closed-toe shoes for walking and climbing. Feet may get injured in sandals.

🍁 Follow the walker's path or bike path.

🍁 Observe the animal life.

🍁 Ask parents to help you organize a picnic lunch and cooperative games.

🍁 Bring children's insect repellent, sunscreen, and a first-aid kit.

🍁 Ask parents to apply sunscreen on their children before coming to school to avoid allergic reactions.

Miniature Parks

Give each child a large sheet of brown construction paper. Set out various tree shapes cut from green construction paper. Let the children glue trees in their parks.

Cut out magazine pictures of people and some small animals you might see in a park. Let the children glue these pictures on their miniature park scenes.

Playground Imagination Mural

Mount a large sheet of butcher paper on the wall. Talk with the children about the kinds of things they would want in an imaginary park filled with wonderful things! Encourage the children's imaginations. Then pass out crayons and let the children draw what they would want in a park on the mural paper. Post this colorful display for parents to see.

Related Books

The Cloud Book, Tomie dePaola, (Holiday, 1975).

The Real Hole, Beverly Cleary, (Morrow, 1986).

We Went Looking, Aileen Fisher, (Crowell, 1968).

Who Lives Here?, Dot and Sy Barlowe, (Random House, 1978).

Park

Fitness Fun

Lead the children along a "physical fitness" path that might be set up at a park. Let the children walk in a line behind you. Have them stop periodically and lead them in a simple exercise—jumping jacks, toe touches, and knee bends.

(To take the children outdoors for this activity in a safe, fun way, let them form a line and hold onto a long clothesline with one hand!)

Park Ranger for the Day

Talk with the children about national parks that are home to wild animals—bears, moose, deer. Set up a corner with stuffed animals, hiking boots, and hats. Let the children take turns being the park ranger for the day and caring for the toy animals.

Park Animal Match-Up

Cut out magazine pictures of animals that wouldn't live in national parks (cats, dogs, gerbils, milk cows) and wild animals that would live in national parks (squirrels, chipmunks, bears, moose, deer). Mount each picture on a sturdy piece of paper. Let the children sort the pictures into two groups—"Animals Found in a Park" and "Animals Not Found in a Park." Let the children share with their classmates how they grouped the animals.

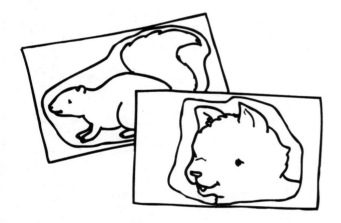

If You're Walking in the Park

Sung to: "If You're Happy and You Know It"

If you're walking in the park,
Shout, "Hooray!" *Hooray!*
If you're walking in the park,
Shout, "Hooray!" *Hooray!*
If you're walking in the park,
Then you're happy as a lark.
If you're walking in the park,
Shout, "Hooray!" *Hooray!*

Marsha Elyn Wright

Have the children walk in a circle as they sing this song.

Cloud Snacks

One fun activity to do at the park is observe the shapes of clouds. Take your children outside and let them observe clouds. Talk about what the shapes look like—bears, elephants, birds, etc. Then set out small paper cups filled with cottage cheese. Let the children arrange the cottage cheese in cloud shapes on paper plates. Let the children eat their cloud shapes with pineapple chunks, apple slices, raisins, and other goodies.

Pet Store

This is always a favorite field trip for young children and is a good experience any time of the year. Most store owners will welcome the children. Look for a store with fish, birds, reptiles, and mammals.

Tips

 Prepare the children by explaining what they will be seeing. Teach them how to approach strange animals.

 If the store has a grooming area, arrange a demonstration of a dog getting a bath and haircut.

 If possible, purchase a pet for the school. Or, purchase food or supplies for a pet you already have at home or school.

 Ask to have a reptile demonstration so the children can learn about the various kinds of reptiles.

 Be sure to spend some time comparing the pet supplies. For example, compare a break-away cat collar to a leather dog collar.

 Talk with your children about the different kinds of pets. List their names. Challenge the children to find all the pets listed.

 Tell your children to keep their hands to themselves for safety.

Charting the Needs of Pets

Make a chart. List the needs of pets. Illustrate each need with a drawing or picture. Read the chart together daily.

Needs of Pets

LOVE

FOOD

CLEAN WATER

EXERCISE

MEDICAL CARE

SHELTER

Pet Shop Corner

Set up a pet shop in a center. Place stuffed animals, plastic baskets, brushes, combs, baby blankets, and pet dishes at the center. Let the children take turns working at the store and shopping at the store. Talk about the different pets they "bought."

Related Books

Ms. Pea's Pet Store & Other Children's Tales, Rachel L. Perez, (Vantage Press, 1995).

Pet Shop Mouse, Judie Schrecker, (Winston-Derek, 1994).

Pet Show, Ezra Jack Keats, (Simon & Schuster, 1974).

Pet Store, M.T. Coffin, (Demco Media, 1996).

Pet Store vol.13, M.T. Coffin, (Avon Books, 1996).

Pet Store

Pet Matching

Cut out magazine pictures of common pets. Write the name of each pet on a sentence strip. Let the children help you match the name with the pet. Make a bulletin board or poster with pictures and their labels.

Pets and Supplies Game

Display magazine pictures of pets on a bulletin board. Cut out pictures of animal homes (birdcages, doghouses, cat beds) and pet supplies (dog food, cat food, dog brush, cat comb, birdseed, and animal toys). Let the children take turns matching each pet to the place where it could live or to the supplies it might need.

Stuffed Animal Pet Show

Have a pet show using stuffed animals. Make sure each pet gets a prize. Let each child have a chance to tell the name of his or her pet and something about it.

Animal Snacks

Set out a variety of animal-shaped snacks—fish-shaped crackers and animal cookies. Let the children snack away!

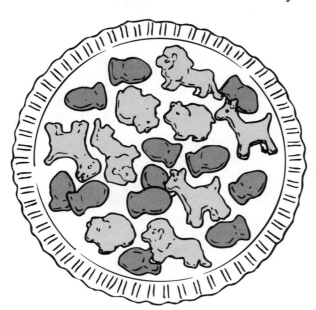

Oh, My Puppy

Sung to: "Clementine"

Bought a puppy,
Bought a puppy,
Bought a puppy just now.
I just now bought a puppy,
Bought a puppy just now.

Took it home,
Took it home,
Took it home just now.
I just now took it home,
Took it home just now.

Fed my puppy,
Fed my puppy.
Fed my puppy just now,
I just now fed my puppy,
Fed my puppy just now.

Marsha Elyn Wright

Have the children help you make up verses to this song to create a funny story.

Plant Nursery

Plants and nursery supplies are more in abundance in the fall or spring. Try to find a business that has a greenhouse, garden vegetables, and flowering plants. Some garden shops will have fountains, water gardens, and wind chimes. These items are always interesting.

Tips

🌸 Teach the children to look and not touch or smell unless they have permission.

🌸 Check if any of your children have allergies to certain plants and insects. Be prepared if you have a child with an insect allergy that may require immediate treatment.

🌸 Purchase some seeds or plants to use at school.

🌸 Ask for a brief talk about the importance of plants and trees.

Related Books

Growing Vegetable Soup, Lois Ehlert, (Harcourt Brace, 1990).

Vegetable Garden, Douglas Florian, (Harcourt Brace, 1996).

Grandma's Vegetable Garden, Patricia B. Hamiltion, (Scripts Publishing, 1997).

Vegetable Garden, Brigid Gaynor, (Red Jacket Press, 1992).

Vegetable Soup—The Fruit Bowl, Dianne Warren and Susan S. Jones, (Oasis Publishing, 1996).

School Garden

Start a small school garden. Radishes, carrots, green beans, and peas grow quickly and easily in a small space. Put the seeds in a plastic jar that has a shaker top, like a spice jar, add some sand or soil, and let the children shake the seeds into the assigned space. Save the seed package and laminate it, or cover it with clear self-stick paper. Attach the label to a craft stick and poke it in the soil to mark the garden area.

Hint! Old tires filled with dirt make good raised beds for plants and flowers.

Shoe Gardens

Have each child bring an old shoe (or hat) to school. The children can decorate the shoes with paint, buttons, lace, etc. Fill each shoe with soil. Let the children plant seeds or a small plant in the shoes.

Plant Nursery

Vegetable Soup Snack

Let the children make vegetable soup for a snack. Ask parents to donate vegetables. Let the children help you wash and chop up carrots, potatoes, celery, and other tasty vegetables.

Add packages of dry vegetable soup mix to a crock pot of water. Let the children take turns stirring the soup before placing the lid on the pot to cook. The next day, serve vegetable soup and crackers!

Vegetable Prints

Let the children make vegetable prints from potatoes, onions, green peppers, and other vegetables. Cut several different vegetables in half. Allow the vegetables to air dry for about an hour. Place folded paper towels in shallow pans and pour small amounts of different colors of tempera paint on the toweling. Give each child a sheet of white construction paper. Have the children dip the vegetable halves into the paint and then press them on their papers to make prints.

Growing Garden of Children

Tell the children to pretend to be flower seeds and take them outdoors to "plant them" in rows. Tell the children you are going to "water" them so they can grow. Pretend to sprinkle water from a watering can on each child. Tell the children that after they are watered, they can start growing up tall into big, beautiful flowers!

Add to this movement activity by playing music while the "flowers" grow!

I'm a Fresh Vegetable

Sung to: "Little White Duck"

I'm a fresh vegetable,
Growing in a garden,
A fresh vegetable,
Growing in a garden.
I grow and I grow,
So ripe that I crunch.
Come take me home,
For a tasty lunch!
I'm a fresh vegetable,
Picked from the garden,
Yum, yum, yum!

Marsha Elyn Wright

Have the children pretend to be vegetables growing in a garden as they sing this song.

Color Sorting

Set out assorted colors of fruits and vegetables. Place matching colors of paper circles beside the produce. Let the children take turns sorting the fruits and vegetables by color on the paper circles.

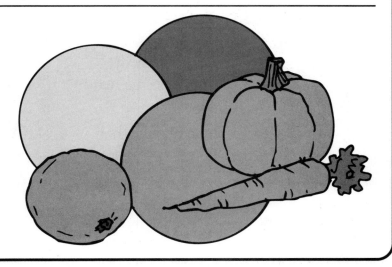

Post Office

February and May are good times to plan a trip to the post office. Lots of cards, letters, and packages are sent for Valentine's Day and Mother's Day!

Tips

- It is important to check with the person who will be leading the group and find out if the post office is prepared to have young children visit.

- Be specific about what you want the children to hear and see. Young children are not interested in ZIP codes or postage rates.

- Young children enjoy seeing inside the mail trucks and watching how the scales work.

- In advance, meet with the person who will lead your group. Ask for permission to take pictures.

- Ask if it would be possible to follow a brightly colored envelope through the mail sorting process. If it is possible, take a large colorful envelope addressed to the school. Follow it from the mail slot to the truck. Most post office personnel will stage this for you if you ask.

Making and Mailing Cards

Let the children make valentines or Mother's Day cards. Give each child a folded sheet of construction paper so it fits inside a business-size envelope. Set out glue, construction paper scraps, markers, lace, and buttons. Let the children decorate their cards. Print for the children what words they wish to say on their cards. Ask parents to send to school self-addressed, stamped, business-size envelopes.

Help the children place their cards in the envelopes and seal them. Walk your children to the post office to mail their cards.

Post Office Center

Set up a pretend post office in a center at school. Have on hand envelopes, writing paper, stickers for stamps, pencils, and a tiny food scale for weighing mail. Let the children play post office—writing, stamping, and sending mail.

Related Books

My Mother the Mail Carrier, Inez Maury, (Feminist Press, 1991).

Never Mail an Elephant, Mike Thaler, (Troll, 1994).

The Post Office Book: Mail and How It Moves, Gail Gibbons, (HarperCollins, 1987).

Tortoise Brings the Mail, Dee Lillegard, (Dutton, 1997).

Post Office

Post Office Book

Make a class big book using the photographs taken at the post office. Let the children dictate words to go under each picture.

Mail Carrier Visit

Ask your area mail carrier to stop at school and visit with the children. Have him or her tell about the uniform, the mail truck, and different ways letters can travel from sender to receiver. Offer a cool or warm drink and some cookies.

Stamp Puzzle

Purchase a blank puzzle with large pieces. Create a simple puzzle design that looks like a stamp. Take apart the pieces and let the children help you put the puzzle together.

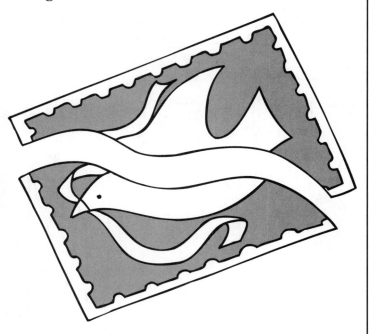

I'm a Little Letter

Sung to: "I'm a Little Teapot"

I'm a little letter,
Set to go.
Here's an envelope,
Just stamp it so.
Drop me in a mailbox,
Ship me out.
Fast I travel.
"Whee!" I shout!

Marsha Elyn Wright

Envelope Sweet Treats

Give each child a business-size envelope. Help the children print their names on the envelopes. Have each child draw a stamp in the corner of the envelope or provide stickers for the children to use. Tell the children to place the envelopes in the "mailbox." (Decorate a cardboard box.) Fill the envelopes with tiny treats and seal. Let the children take turns being the postmaster and delivering the envelope sweet treats to the other children!

Service Station

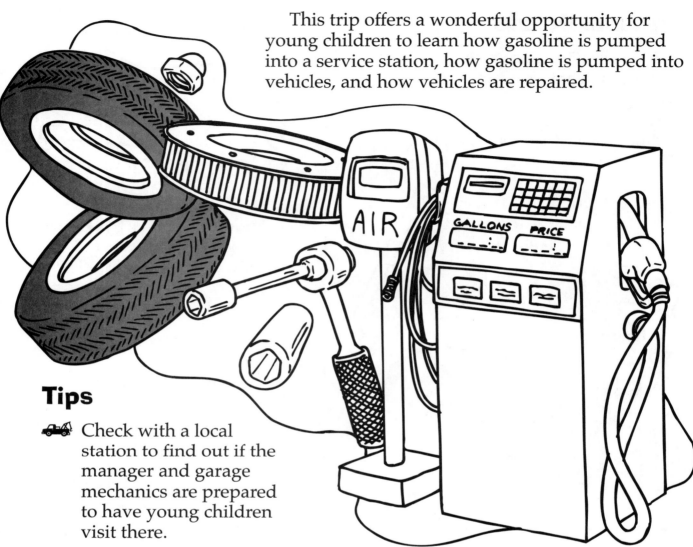

This trip offers a wonderful opportunity for young children to learn how gasoline is pumped into a service station, how gasoline is pumped into vehicles, and how vehicles are repaired.

Tips

- Check with a local station to find out if the manager and garage mechanics are prepared to have young children visit there.

- Ask for a demonstration on how the cash register works and how gasoline is pumped into a car.

- Ask if someone will demonstrate how special equipment works—air pump, air jack, the car hoist, the tire irons, etc.

- If the station has a car wash, ask if the children may watch a car being washed.

- Let the children watch the numbers spin on the gas pump as gasoline is being pumped. Keep the children at a safe distance!

- Ask if someone will talk to the children about how to stay safe when they're at a gas station.

- Talk about the difference between full-serve and self-serve.

Toy Car Wash

Set up a toy car wash in the outside play area. Provide a hose with a nozzle, sponges, pails, wiping rags, wagons, and toy vehicles. Let the children take turns washing and "waxing" vehicles.

Service Station Play

Collect large, tall cardboard boxes, plastic tools, and large toy vehicles. Set up a play service station outdoors. Use paint and markers to transform the boxes into gas pumps, computer diagnostic machines, cashier counter, and other service station equipment. Let the children take turns being customers and mechanics at the station. The customers bring cars and trucks to be fixed or have gas pumped into them, and the mechanics service the vehicles.

Related Books

Cars, James Clark, (Raintree, 1981).

Cars and Trucks and Things That Go, Richard Scarry, (Western, 1951).

I Want to Be a Service Station Attendant, Eugene Baker, (Children's Press, 1972).

What Happens at a Gas Station, Arthur Shay, (Reily and Lee, 1972).

Service Station

Paper Trucks, Cars, and Wheels

Cut out car and truck shapes from various colors of construction paper. Cut out small circles from black construction paper to make wheels for the vehicles. Give each child a sheet of construction paper. Have the children glue vehicles on their papers and then glue wheels on their vehicles. After the children finish their pictures, give them time to share their artwork.

Service Mechanic Visit

Ask a local service station if one of their mechanics could visit your classroom. Ask the mechanic to show the children how to change a tire.

Logo Matching Game

Cut matching pairs of gasoline logos out of magazines. Glue each logo on an index card. Mix them up. Let the children take turns matching up the logos.

Down by the Station

Sung to: "Down by the Station"

Down by the station,
Trucks and cars are waiting.
People pump the gasoline,
Standing in a row.
See the car mechanics,
Fixing up the big trucks.
"Beep, beep,
Honk, honk,"
Off they go!

Marsha Elyn Wright

Cheese and Cracker Car Snacks

Set out small and large slices of different kinds of cheese, round tire-shaped crackers, and pretzel sticks. Let the children transform the cheese slices into trucks and cars with cracker wheels. Have the children use the pretzels to outline the car bodies and add doors and windows. After sharing their creations, let the feast begin!

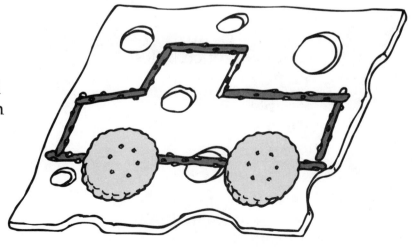

Shell Shop

These shops are usually found in beach front communities. Try to find a shop that has shells and dry fish. A good shop will have shells from all over the world in a variety of colors and sizes.

Tips

- Visit the shop and discuss the possibility for a short talk by the staff. Ask them to name the shells and tell where they came from.

- Remind the children to look but not touch unless given permission.

- If possible, purchase a few shells to take back to school.

- Ask if the staff would talk about local outdoor areas where the children could collect shells.

- Since these shops are usually in beach communities, try to allow time to visit a fish market or to walk along the beach.

- If you go to the beach, stress staying away from the water. Focus on beachcombing. (Life jackets for the children are a good idea any time they are near water.)

Shell Sizes

Purchase about five or six scallop shells in assorted sizes. Make a nesting activity by letting the children take turns stacking the shells from largest to smallest. You can also cut pictures of different size shells out of magazines and glue each picture on an index card. Then have the children arrange the shell pictures by size.

Looking at Shells

Set out assorted shells for the children to explore. Add a pan of water so the children can wet the shells and see the colors.

Related Books

A House for Hermit Crab, Eric Carle, (Simon & Schuster, 1991).

Journey in a Shell, Christiane Renauld, (Childs World, 1991).

The Magic of Sea Shells, Fredlee, (Windward Press, 1986).

Seashell Magic, Phylliss Adams, Carole P. Mitchener, and Virginia Johnson, (Modern Curriculum, 1989).

Shells, S. Peter Dance, (D K Publishing, 1992).

Shells: Treasures of the Sea, Leonard Hill, (Levin, Hugh Lauter Associates, 1996).

Who's in the Shell?, Leslie McGuire, (Readers Digest, 1995).

Shell Shop

Sandcastle Clay

Make sandcastle clay by cooking clean play sand with cornstarch and water. Store in an airtight container until ready to use. Let the children use assorted yogurt and ice cream cups and other disposal containers to mold sand into various shapes. Have the children stack the shapes together to make sandcastles. Let the children decorate the castles with small shells. Small shells are available by the pound at hobby and import shops.

Observing and Sorting Shells

Let the children hold, touch, and feel a variety of shells. Ask the children to describe the different textures, shapes, sizes, and colors. Introduce words such as *smooth, rough, bumpy, shiny,* and *dull.* Then have the children sort the shells in groups according to size, shape, color, or texture.

Digging for Treasure

Hide small seashells in a pan of sand or in the sand table. Let the children "dig for treasure" and try to find the seashells.

I'm a Little Seashell

Sung to: "I'm a Little Teapot"

I'm a little seashell,
Rough and round,
Red, green, and yellow,
Orange, blue, and brown.
There are lots of seashells,
Just like me.
We lay on the beach,
Along the sea!

Marsha Elyn Wright

Crab Salad Snack

Make crab salad for a snack. Check for allergies to seafood before you plan this activity. If there are children with allergies, cook shell-shaped pasta. Then add chopped vegetables and cheese for a different treat!

Television Station

A guided tour is usually available at local television stations. They often have someone assigned to tours. This person will ask what you want to see. Some high schools and colleges also have studios that allow tours.

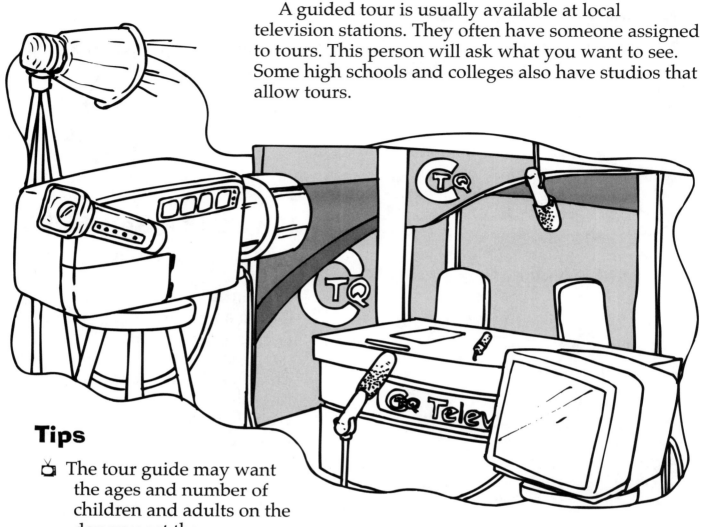

Tips

📺 The tour guide may want the ages and number of children and adults on the day you set the appointment. Have this information available when you place the call.

📺 This is a good summer or winter trip. Stations will be large enough to hold most groups and station staff will be accustomed to giving tours to children.

📺 Prepare the children by telling them what to expect on the tour after you have talked to the staff.

📺 Tell the children that they may see their favorite local newsperson.

📺 Tell the children to remain as quiet as possible in the newsrooms when people are using the phones or are recording.

📺 Ask if someone will demonstrate how a television camera works.

Smile for the Camera!

Let the children take turns being classroom news reporters. Let the reporter wear a toy camera around his or her neck and pretend to take pictures of his or her classmates doing school activities. If you have the resources, purchase a roll of film for the camera and let each reporter take one or two actual photographs. Develop the photos and display them for all to see. Let the children try to identify which photographs they took!

Video Fun

Videotape your children. Show the video on television at school.

Related Books

The Berenstain Bears' Media Madness, Stan and Jan Berenstain, (Random House, 1995).

Let's Visit a Television Station, Carol Freed, (Troll, 1988).

Local News, Gary Soto, (Scholastic, 1994).

Working at a TV Station, Gary Davis, (Children's Press, 1998).

Television Station

Weather Matching

Talk with your children about what a weather forecaster does. Ask if anyone has seen a weather report on television.

Then cut out magazine pictures of five different weather conditions—rainy, snowy, sunny, windy, and cloudy. Mount each picture on a sheet of construction paper. Talk with the children about the five different kinds of weather. Draw on separate index cards a simple weather symbol for each kind of weather—raindrops, snowflakes, a sun, something blowing in the wind, and a puffy cloud. Let the children take turns matching the weather pictures with the weather symbols.

Television Play

Make a play television camera out of a large cardboard box or take everything out of an old wooden television. Let the children take turns pretending to be part of a television show while the rest of the children are watching.

Ready, Set, Action!

Make a play television camera out of a cardboard box, toilet paper and wrapping paper tubes, tape, and markers. Set the camera on a tall stool or let the children using the camera hold it in their hands.

Have the children take turns being a camera person who "films" the rest of the class retelling a story or acting out a simple skit.

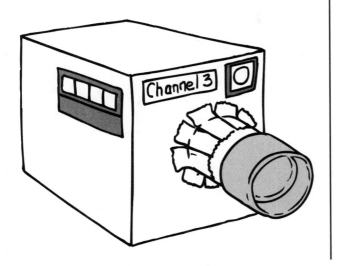

When You Watch a TV Show

Sung to: "Twinkle, Twinkle, Little Star"

When you watch a TV show,
You can learn a lot, I know.
How to care for pets and trees,
How to keep away from bees,
Watching TV can be fun,
You'll learn a lot
Before you're done!

Marsha Elyn Wright

Popcorn Snack Time

Place popcorn in small lunch sacks. Pass out the snack bags to the children and let them munch while they watch a children's video.

Veterinary Hospital

There may be several possibilities for this trip. Some veterinarian practices only take small animals, others take only farm animals, and some take both. Try to find the ones that treat both kinds of animals. Make sure the staff is willing to schedule time to guide the children through the facility.

Tips

🐰 Gather as much information as possible about the local veterinarians before you select one. If you have a pet and use a local veterinarian, start with the doctor you know.

🐰 Prepare the children for the smells they may encounter.

🐰 Check to see if any of the children are allergic to dogs and cats.

🐰 Tell the children that if there is an emergency while they are visiting, their tour may be shortened if the emergency requires all the staff.

🐰 Ask if the clinic has any resident animals that could be given a brief medical exam while the children are visiting. Many of the instruments vets use are similar to those doctors use on children.

🐰 Ask if the tour can include the office, the examination room, the kennel, the medical lab, the surgery room, the X-ray room, and if they care for livestock, the large animal pens.

Veterinarian Office Play

Set up a veterinarian's office at school using stuffed animals, baby blankets, doll beds, and toy medical supplies from doctors' kits. Let the children take turns being the doctor and medical staff as well as the clients with sick pets.

Pet Chart

Discuss different ways to keep pets safe and healthy. Make a chart showing the needs of pets. Cut out several magazine pictures of different pets. Let the children mount the pictures on the chart. Read the chart daily.

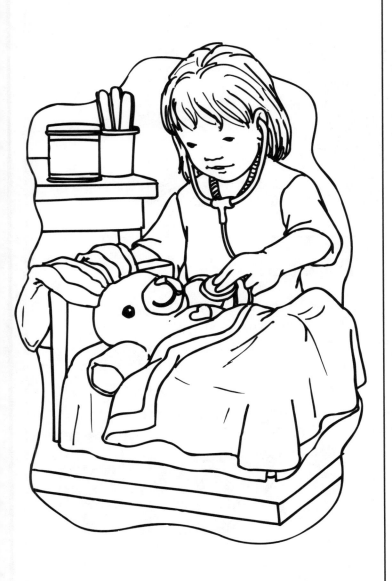

Related Books

My Mom's a Vet, Henry Horenstein, (Candlewick Press, 1996).

Dixie and Strip, Gilbert Morris, (Moody Press, 1998).

Pets, Vets, and Mary Howard, Joan Davenport Carris, (HarperCollins, 1987).

Down Dairy Farm Road, C.L. Martin and C.L.G. Martin, (Simon & Schuster, 1994).

"Visiting a Vet" Class Book

Let each child draw and color a picture of a favorite part of the field trip. Record for each child what he or she would like to say about the trip. Write the words below each drawing. Bind the pages to make a class book. Let the children take turns sharing the book with their parents.

A Pet Visits

Bring in a small dog, cat, or guinea pig. Teach the children the proper way to handle the small animals. Let each child draw a picture of the visiting pet to share with family members.

Pet Tags

Talk with the children about the importance of identifying tags for pets that provide the pet's name and the telephone number of the owner. Then let the children choose dog or cat names for themselves. Print each child's name on a piece of construction paper cut in the shape of a bone or a heart. Let the children decorate their tags and wear them around their necks all day!

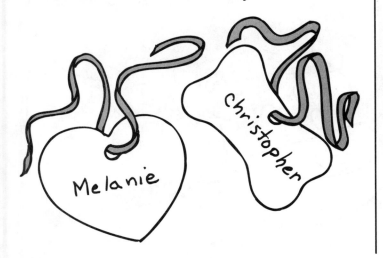

Dogs and Cats

Sung to: "This Old Man"

Dogs and cats,
Need our care,
Food and shelter,
Love we share,
With exercise,
And a toy that they can chew,
Dogs and cats,
Will sure love you!

Marsha Elyn Wright

Animal Cracker Snacks

Give each child a box of animal crackers. Have the children line up their crackers and see how many animals they can name. Talk about the difference between pets and wild animals. Then let the children eat their animal snacks!

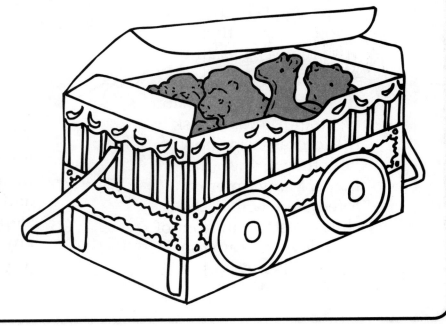

Weather Station

There is a possibility of having several locations for this kind of field trip depending on where you live. You could visit a national weather station, a regional weather station, a major university with a meteorology department, or a broadcasting station that trains weather forecasters for television work.

SUNDAY	80
MONDAY	79
TUESDAY	75
WEDNESDAY	78
THURSDAY	80
FRIDAY	84
SATURDAY	88

Tips

☔ Try to plan this trip during a calm weather time of the year when the weather person is not busy tracking major storms or floods.

☔ Prepare the children for being in busy offices with many wires and computers.

☔ If you choose a television weather forecaster, ask the forecaster to show how they use weather maps. Many times, forecasters will let the children stand in front of the television camera and see themselves on the monitors.

☔ Ask the forecaster to not be too technical for such young children.

☔ Remind the children to keep their hands to themselves and to watch where they step so as not to trip over any wires or cables.

☔ Ask for a demonstration of a weather balloon.

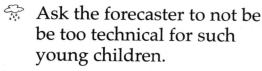

Mini Weather Station

Set up a mini weather station at school with simple maps, charts, and pictures. Cut these out of magazines and newspapers. Each day, help the children observe, record, and graph the temperature, weather conditions, and wind directions.

Related Books

The Cloud Book, Tomie dePaola, (Holiday House, 1984).

It Looks Like Spilt Milk, Charles G. Shaw, (HarperCollins, 1993).

Little Cloud, Eric Carle, (Putman, 1998).

Studying Weather, Ann and Jim Merk, (Rourke Cor., 1994).

Weather, Lee Bennett Hopkins, (HarperCollins, 1994).

The Weather: Sun, Rain, Wind, Snow, Colleen Carroll, (Abbeville Press, 1998).

World of Weather, David A. Adler, (Troll, 1989).

Tissue Rainbows

Talk with your children about what kind of weather creates a rainbow—rain and sunshine. Tell the children if they want to see a rainbow on a rainy day when the sun is shining, they need to stand with their backs to the sun and their faces toward the rain. Share how a rainbow is really round. It forms a circle around the earth, but we see only a part of it.

Then set out sheets of red, orange, yellow, green, blue, and purple tissue paper. Have each child brush an arc of liquid starch on a sheet of white construction paper. Tell the children to tear pieces of the red tissue paper and press them on the arc. Tell the children to brush another arc below the first arc, making the two arcs touch. Have the children tear orange pieces of tissue and press it on the second arc just below the red arc. The red and orange tissue pieces should overlap a bit. To complete the rainbows, have the children repeat this procedure for the colors yellow, green, blue, and purple, in that order.

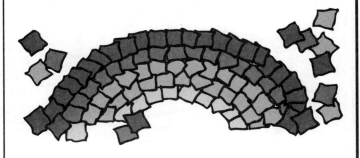

Weather Station

Windsocks

Windsocks show the direction of the wind. Let the children make their own windsocks. Give each child an oatmeal container with the top and bottom cut off and a precut piece of construction paper to fit around the outside of the container. Have the children color designs on their papers and help them glue the papers around the outside of the containers. Cut long strips of colored cellophane. Staple strips around one end of each container. Poke three holes at the other end of each container and tie a string through each hole. Tie the loose ends together.

Take the children outdoors on a windy day. Let the children hold up their windsocks to see in which direction the wind is blowing!

Rain, Rain, Rain

Make rain! Boil water in a pot until steam forms to make a "cloud." Fill a shallow pan with ice cubes and hold it above the steam cloud. Have your children watch what happens when the steam comes in contact with the cool air from the pan—water droplets form on the bottom of the pan and fall back into the pot like rain!

Tornado in a Bottle

Fill one 2-liter plastic bottle half full of water. Place another 2-liter plastic bottle on top of the first bottle so the neck openings touch. Securely tape together the neck openings. Move the bottles in a circular motion so the water in the bottom bottle swirls in a circle. Immediately turn the bottles so the water-filled bottle is on top of the empty bottle. Let the children watch the "tornado" that forms as the water flows from one bottle to the other.

Take your children outside and let them move in the wind like swirling tornadoes!

Wind Is Blowing

Sung to: "Frère Jacques"

Wind is blowing,
Wind is blowing,
All around,
All around,
Puffy clouds are swirling,
Tiny leaves are twirling,
In the air,
In the air.

Marsha Elyn Wright

Tornado Chocolate Drinks

Fill paper cups with milk, one for each child. Give each child a plastic spoon and a cup of milk. Pour some chocolate syrup in each cup of milk. Let the children make "tornadoes" by swirling the milk in a circle with their spoons. Serve this delicious drink with cookies during snack time.

Wildlife Refuge

This trip can be the best trip of the year, but it is potentially the most challenging and requires the most planning. Schedule this trip in the late fall or early spring when animals have less cover from the trees.

Tips

- Visit the site. Ask if there is an exhibit area of preserved animals. If there is, show the children this area first so they will know what they are trying to find.

- Ask if guided tours are available or if the tour is self-guided. If it is self-guided, ask for a map and for information to help you identify the animals and their tracks.

- Ask the staff where they would suggest you take your group. Take the map, a highlighter, a pen, and a notebook. Visit each location and make notes. Judge the amount of time you have with the stops that are available.

- Ask if clean, running water is available in the restrooms. If water isn't available, take plenty of fresh water with you.

- As you visit each area, look for animals or signs of animals like droppings, tracks, feathers, and nests. Tell the children they will only see animals if they are quiet. Teach them to look for signs of animals and remind them not to disturb any signs they find.

- Do a practice walk at school. Stress being very quiet and learning hand signals to point out things you see.

🦌 Be prepared! You will be visiting an area with wild animals, even though most of these animals are familiar with people. During mating and birthing seasons, they may be more aggressive or protective. They may also be aggressive if injured or scared. Be alert for swarms of insects. Watch for snakes on the ground.

🦌 Pack a backpack with a first-aid kit, instant ice cold pack, at least a quart of drinkable water, tissues, and insect bite medication. Take colored tape or cloth strips to mark the trails if there is a chance you will get lost.

🦌 Take one adult for every three or four children.

🦌 The leader should wear a whistle. (Teach the children that the whistle sound is a signal for everyone to freeze. Danger is near, or someone is in a dangerous place.)

🦌 Send home a note requiring special clothes for the trip. Everyone (adults and children) must wear long pants, sturdy shoes with closed toes, mid-calf socks, long-sleeved shirts, and a hat. Everyone must tuck their pant legs inside their socks. This keeps ticks, red bugs, and other insects from crawling up pant legs. Ask the parents to spray insect repellent on the pants, socks, shoes, and shirts before the children come to school.

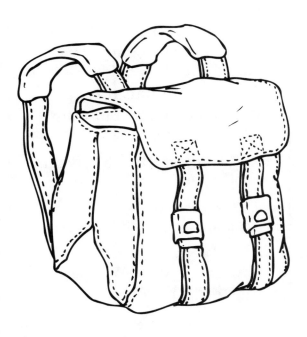

Wildlife Refuge

Tips continued

- If any child is allergic to insect bites, take his or her medication in the backpack.

- Depending on the site and the distance from school, you may want to take snacks and juice, or even a picnic lunch, for the children. Take some extra clothes like long-sleeved shirts (in case someone has an accident or gets dirty) and plastic bags for muddy shoes.

- Don't forget a camera!

Mini First-Aid Kits

Let each child make a mini first-aid kit. Have the children decorate the outside of plastic film canisters with nature stickers. Let each child place a few small adhesive bandages and some wrapped germ wipe towels inside his or her kit. This mini kit fits easily in a pocket. Teach the children to be prepared when away from home.

Related Books

Aransas: A Naturalist Guide, Wayne H. and Martha K. McAlister, (University of Texas Press, 1995).

Places of Refuge: Our National Wildlife Refuge System, Dorothy Hinshaw Patent, (Houghton Mifflin, 1992).

A Walk in the Wild: Exploring a Wildlife Refuge, Lorraine Ward, (Charlesbridge, 1993).

Wildlife ABC, Jan Thornhill, (Firefly Books, 1996).

Wildlife Homes, Neil Morris, (Readers Digest, 1994).

Wildlife Refuge: A Classroom Adventure, Lorraine Wood, (Charlesbridge, 1997).

Trail Mix Snack

Let the children help you make trail mix using granola cereal, raisins, chocolate chips, nuts, and dried fruits. Have each child scoop some mix into a self-sealing plastic bag. Write each child's name in permanent marker on the bag. Let the children eat their snack outside in the play area.

Oh, I'm Hiking

Sung to: "Clementine"

Oh, I'm hiking,
Oh, I'm hiking,
Oh, I'm hiking up and down,
Drinking water,
Eating trail mix,
As I hike so far from town!

Marsha Elyn Wright

Wild Animal Sorting

Cut out magazine pictures of wild animals that the children might see in a wildlife refuge— ducks, birds, squirrels, snakes. Talk with the children about the sizes, colors, habitats, and other attributes of the animals. Let the children help you sort the animals by size, color, or other attribute. Mix up the pictures and sort them again by a different attribute.

X-ray Lab

This trip is fun around Halloween when playful skeletons are part of household decorations. Seeing the large X-ray equipment will make your children less afraid of getting an X-ray when they are injured.

Tips

+ Send a note home explaining what kind of experience you want for your children. Ask parents to recommend an X-ray lab that has a staff which works well with children. Parents may have a friend or relative who works in a lab or doctor's office with X-ray equipment.

+ Contact the lab and the recommended person. Tell this person about your group. Schedule a day and time when the staff will be able to demonstrate some equipment. Be flexible and go when the lab has time for your group.

+ Ask if the lab will display a variety of X-rays of different body parts for the children to observe.

+ Ask for a demonstration of how people are placed in front of or inside the equipment.

+ Prepare the children. Tell them that no one will be given an X-ray.

+ Remind the children that they need to be quiet, keep their hands to themselves, and to not push any buttons!

Studying Skeletons

If you have had an X-ray, you can request to have it from your doctor. (Labs cannot give away X-rays.) Display it for the children to see. Buy a full-size paper skeleton at a party store or see if you can borrow a plastic skeleton from your doctor's office. Talk with your children about the major bones—spine, backbone, hipbone, and arm and leg bones. Help the children compare what they see on the X-ray to the skeleton.

Making Skeletons

Set out glue, scissors, craft sticks, toothpicks, and straws. Give each child a sheet of black construction paper. Have the children make skeletons by arranging the craft sticks, the toothpicks, or the straws on the black paper. Let the children share their skeleton creations!

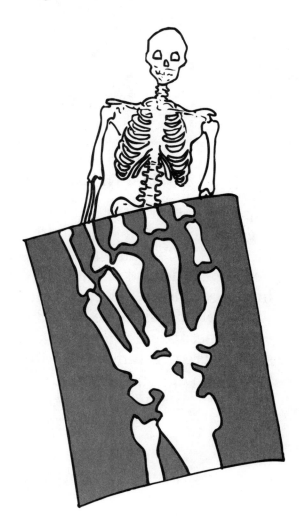

Related Books

Bones, Seymour Simon, (William Morrow, 1998).

Skeletons and Movement, Maria Gordan, (Raintree, 1995).

The X-ray Picture Book of Amazing Animals, Gerald Legg and David Salariya, (Franklin Watts, 1994).

X-rays and Other Fun Things, Richard Scarry, (Simon & Schuster, 1998).

X-ray Lab

Skeleton Puzzle Game

Find a picture of a skeleton and make a copy of it. Laminate both skeleton pictures or cover them with clear self-stick paper. Make a puzzle game. Cut up one skeleton picture into large puzzle pieces. Let the children take turns putting the puzzle together. Have the children place the cut-out pieces on top of the whole picture to make a complete skeleton puzzle.

Bones Are Important

Tape dowel rods or craft sticks to a rag doll to make a simplified model of a skeletal frame. This will help hold the doll's arms and legs in place. Tell the children that without a skeleton, their bodies would act like rag dolls, unable to stand or reach. Tell the children that the skeleton protects the body's brain and other organs.

Simon Says

Play the favorite game of "Simon Says" with your children. As you play the game, have the children touch different "bones" of their bodies. For example, Simon says, "Touch your toe bones" or Simon says, "Touch your hipbone."

Head and Shoulders

Head and shoulders,
Knees and toes,
Knees and toes,
Head and shoulders,
Knees and toes,
Knees and toes,
Eyes and ears
    and mouth and nose,
Head and shoulders,
Knees and toes,
Knees and toes!

Traditional

Have the children point to their body parts as they sing!

Sweet Feet Treats

Cream together a 3-ounce package of softened cream cheese; dried blueberries, cherries, or other small fruit; and a few tablespoons of unsweetened, frozen orange juice concentrate. Have the children wash their hands. Let the children scoop out some of the mixture onto paper plates. Have the children form foot shapes out of the mixture and then eat this sweet feet treat!

Zoo

Your children will be delighted to walk through the zoo and look at the animals! You should be able to request a special program from the zoo staff. You might be able to tour the food preparation area and nursery where the animal babies are sometimes kept.

Tips

 Call your nearest zoo and see what kinds of guided tours they offer for young children.

Ask for special school rates.

Ask when the best time of the year is to visit. Choose a time when there is a limited number of school groups at the zoo. Late spring is usually a crowded time at the zoo.

Take extra adults if the zoo is large—one adult to four children, if possible.

Remind your children to keep their hands out of cages and to not climb on rocks and railings.

Ask if snacks can be brought in the zoo for the children. If food is allowed, take snacks and plan a time to rest, to eat, and to go to the restrooms.

If this is a large zoo, plan to bring sack lunches. Make sure each child's name is printed on his or her sack. Bring extra snacks and drinks for children with big appetites!

Zoo Banners

Cut out several large, pennant-shaped pieces of construction paper in a variety of colors. Display lots of pictures of zoo animals. Talk with your children about the different animals they can see at the zoo. Let each child decorate a pennant so it looks similar to the zoo banners sold in gift shops. Help the children print their words.

Zoo Map

Mount a large sheet of butcher paper on a wall. Draw a simple map of the zoo on the mural. Talk with your children about the different areas and label them. Let the children tape magazine pictures of zoo animals in their appropriate areas on the map. Talk with your children about which zoo animals they like seeing the best!

Related Books

At the Zoo, Judith E. Rinard, (National Geographic Society, 1993).

A Children's Zoo, Tana Hoban, (Greenwillow, 1985).

Nighttime at the Zoo, Dale Smith, (Golden Anchor Press, 1997).

Polar Bear, Polar Bear, What Do You Hear?, Bill Martin, (Henry Holt,

Zoo

Zoo Animal Cookies

Prepare a simple sugar cookie dough and refrigerate to chill the dough. Have the children wash their hands. Give each child a ball of dough to flatten to about ¼-inch thick. (Ask parents to bring rolling pins from home for their children to use.)

Let the children use different zoo animal cookie cutters to press into the dough. Bake. Let cool and eat!

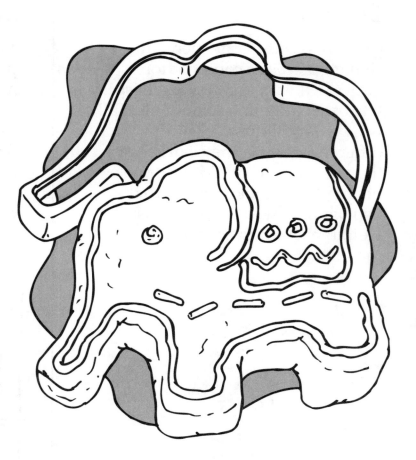

Animal Pictures

Collect a variety of magazine and calendar pictures of zoo animals. Lay them facedown on a table. Let the children take turns turning over a picture and identifying the animal. Ask the rest of the children to tell one thing they know about the animal—what it eats, where it sleeps, what sound it makes, what size it is, etc.

Animal Pictures

Have the children form a circle. Ask for a volunteer to stand in the center of the circle and pretend to be a zoo animal. Have the center child move and make sounds like the animal he or she chose. The rest of the children try to guess the name of the animal. Whoever guesses correctly gets to be in the center. If the guesser has already had a turn, he or she chooses someone else to be in the center.

At the Zoo

Sung to: "The Wheels on the Bus"

The tigers at the zoo
Go *roar, roar, roar,*
Roar, roar, roar,
Roar, roar, roar.
The tigers at the zoo
Go *roar, roar, roar,*
As they feed and play.

The monkeys at the zoo
Go *screech, screech, screech,*
Screech, screech, screech,
Screech, screech, screech.
The monkeys at the zoo
Go *screech, screech, screech,*
As they feed and play.

Marsha Elyn Wright

Have the children help you make up verses to this song!

Zoo Food Snacks

Talk with the children about the different fruits many zoo animals eat—oranges, apples, grapes, bananas. Then slice up some "zoo food" and let the children snack on the different varieties of fruits.

Thank-You Posters for Any Field Trip

Let the children show their appreciation for the field trip leaders by creating a thank-you poster for each trip. Stress the importance of thanking people. Encourage the children to draw thank-you cards whenever they want to thank someone at school or at home. Set up a writing center with a supply of folded construction paper cards, markers, rubber stamps and ink pads, stickers, paper scraps, scissors, and glue.

How to Make a Thank-You Poster

1. With the children, write a thank-you letter to the person who guided you on your field trip. Print your letter on a sheet of writing paper. If the children are able, let them sign their names to the group letter. Read the letter back to the children.

2. Give each child a 4" x 6" index card. Have each child draw a picture of something he or she learned from the trip on it. Encourage details. Ask each child to tell you about his or her drawing and record their words on the card. Write the child's name and age in the corner of the card.

3. Mount the class letter in the center of a large sheet of colored posterboard. Let the children mount their cards around the class letter. Show the finished poster to your children. Read all their quotes.

4. Mail the poster in a mailing tube or deliver it in person to the location.

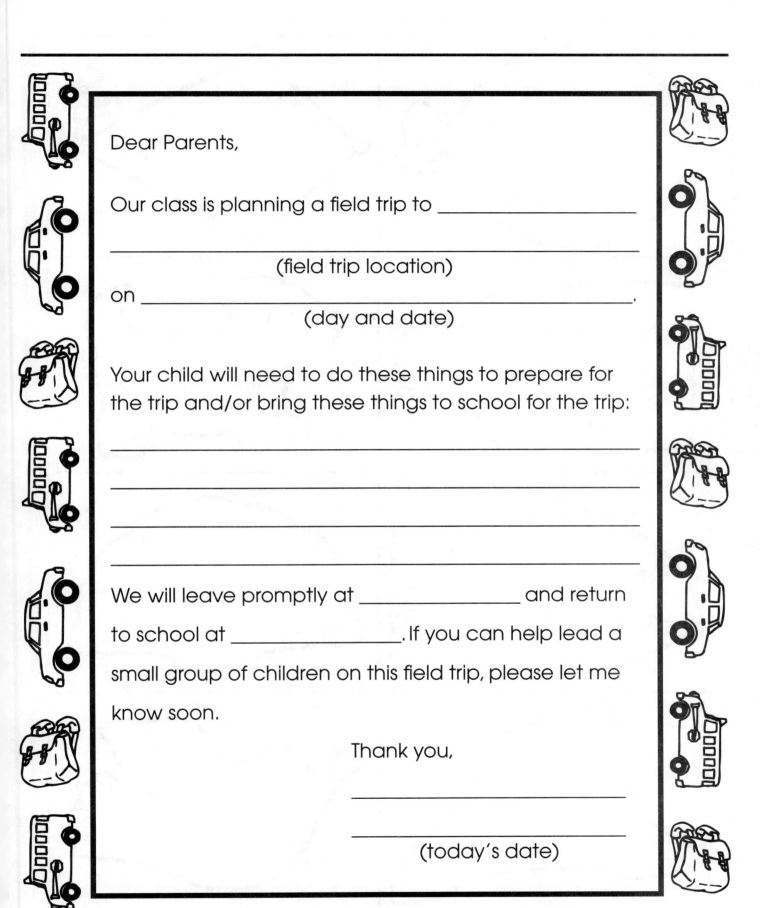

Dear Parents,

Our class is planning a field trip to _____

_____
(field trip location)

on _____.
(day and date)

Your child will need to do these things to prepare for the trip and/or bring these things to school for the trip:

_____

_____

_____

_____

We will leave promptly at _____ and return

to school at _____. If you can help lead a

small group of children on this field trip, please let me

know soon.

Thank you,

_____

_____
(today's date)

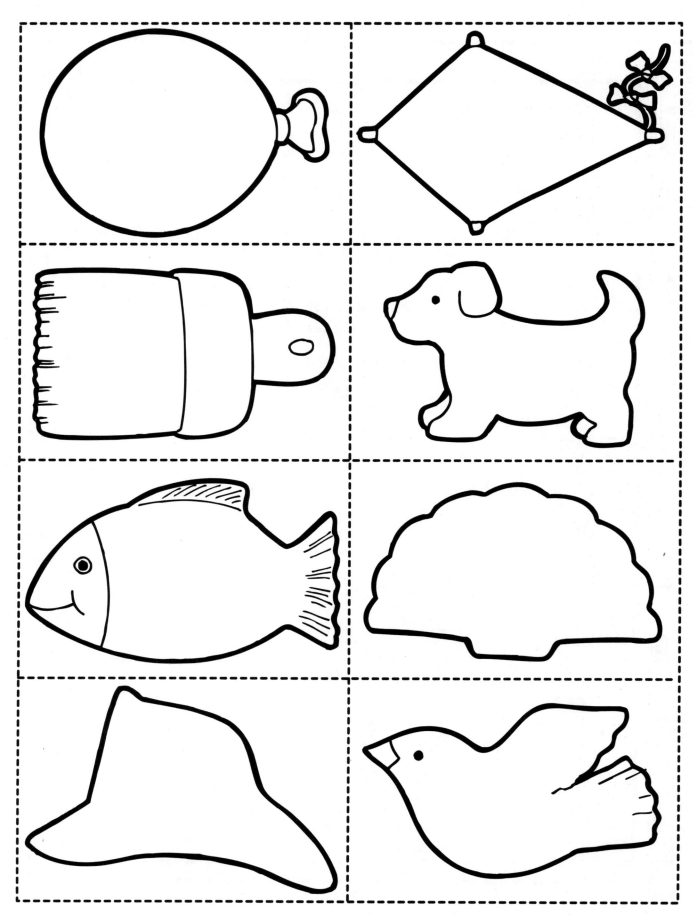

Teacher: Copy these name tags to use on field trips with your children. Let each child decorate one.